The Fragility of Goodness

By the same author

Facing the Extreme
On Human Diversity
The Morals of History
Voices from the Gulag

The Fragility of Goodness
Why Bulgaria's Jews Survived the Holocaust

A COLLECTION OF TEXTS WITH COMMENTARY BY

TZVETAN TODOROV

Translated by Arthur Denner

Princeton University Press
Princeton and Oxford

Published in the United States and the Philippine Islands by Princeton University
Press, 41 William Street, Princeton, New Jersey 08540

First published in English by Weidenfeld & Nicolson, London and in French by
Albin Michel, France.

Library of Congress Control Number 2001088186

ISBN 0-691-08832-2

This book has been composed in Janson

Printed on acid-free paper. ∞

www.pup.princeton.edu

Printed in the United States of America

10 9 8 7 6 5 4 3 2 1

Contents

Introduction   1
The Sequence of Events   3
Memories in Competition   14
Why and How   27

Documents
Exclusion   43

1 Statement by the Bulgarian Writers' Union to the
  Prime Minister and the Chairman of the National
  Assembly   45
2 Statement by the Governing Board of the Bulgarian
  Lawyers' Union to the Chairman of the National
  Assembly   47
3 Open Letter from Christo Punev to the National
  Assembly Deputies   50
4 Statement by the Holy Synod of the Bulgarian
  Orthodox Church to the Prime Minister   54
5 Open Letter from Dimo Kazasov to the
  Prime Minister   58
6 Petko Stainov's Speech in the National Assembly   62
7 Todor Polyakov's Speech in the National Assembly   65

Deportation   71

1 Article from the *Fatherland Front*   73

2 A Leaflet of the Sofia District Committee of the
   Workers' Party   75
3 Protest Letter by the Vice-Chairman of the 25th
   Session of the National Assembly, Dimitâr Peshev,
   and Forty-two Other Deputies   78
4 Petko Stainov's Interrogatory, Sent to the
   Prime Minister and Minister of Foreign Affairs,
   Bogdan Filov   81
5 Bogdan Filov's Diary   84
6 Charles Rédard's Report to the Federal Political
   Department in Berne   92

Internment   95

1 Minutes of a Special Session of the Holy Synod   97
2 Protocol No. 9, 6 June 1943, on King Boris's
   Speech to the Small Cabinet of the Holy Synod   102
3 Letter from Nikola Mushanov and Petko Stainov
   to King Boris   104
4 Letter from Public Figures to King Boris   106
5 'Mad Assault against the Jews': An Article from the
   Workers' Cause   108

Memoirs   113

1 Dimo Kazasov   117
2 Metropolitan Stefan   125
3 Asen Suichmezov   132
4 Dimitâr Peshev   137

Bibliographical Note   185
Translator's Note   187
Index   189

Introduction

The past century will go down in history as one in which mass violence reached levels the world had never before known. The persecution and annihilation of Europe's Jews surely constitute one of the most tragic episodes in human history. Yet these events also offer us the opportunity – a rare one, unfortunately – to see, in the efforts made by some to help the persecuted and save those living under threat of death, how goodness can flourish too. Acts of goodness occur sporadically almost everywhere; but there are two countries that can recall their history with pride, thanks to the collective protection they provided the Jews while themselves living under German control. These two countries are Denmark and Bulgaria. At the time that the Red Army was nearing the Bulgarian frontier, writes Hannah Arendt in *Eichmann in Jerusalem*, 'not a single Bulgarian Jew had been deported or had died an unnatural death . . . I know of no attempt,' she adds, 'to explain the conduct of the Bulgarian people, which is unique in the belt of mixed populations.'

How can we understand this miraculous occurence of goodness? Did these peoples possess exceptional moral and political qualities? As far as the Bulgarians are concerned, I know at first hand that they do not hold themselves in particularly high regard. Of course they love their land and cherish their memories, but when it comes to making value judgments, they are quick to maintain that other peoples, both near and far, are superior. Apart from rare moments of patriotic fervour, they are not in the habit of thinking of themselves as heroes. Thus it was with some astonishment on their part that they discovered this heroic chapter in their own history.

The present volume was conceived as an attempt to explain this fortunate outcome. What exactly happened in Bulgaria during these war years? Is it true that all of Bulgaria's Jews were saved? Who were the protagonists and what motivated them? How did they go about doing what they did? I have sought answers to these questions in the documents and memoirs concerning these events, some of which have been translated within these covers; the answers I have found I offer here as well. But first, let us recall a few pages from the history books.*

---

*Bibliographical references can be found on p. 185. Throughout the book, the transliteration of Bulgarian words follows the Library of Congress Bulgarian transliteration system, except in proper names, where the most common version of the same name in English or the closest phonetic equivalent is adopted.

The Sequence of Events

The history of the persecution and protection of the Jews of Bulgaria is well known, having been the subject of a number of studies, notably since Frederick Chary's landmark work *The Bulgarian Jews and the Final Solution*, published in 1972; various studies that have come out since have clarified certain details. I will therefore confine myself to recalling the major events in this episode.

Three elements of the historical and demographic context must be taken into consideration at the outset.

The first is that, at the end of the Second Balkan War (1913) and again at the conclusion of the First World War (1914–18), Bulgaria had to give up several provinces inhabited partly by Bulgarian populations: Dobrudja was ceded to Romania, Thrace to Greece, and Macedonia to Serbia, the future Yugoslavia. The hope of restoring these provinces to Bulgarian control was still very much alive in Bulgaria at the beginning of the Second World War.

The second element concerns the political situation within Bulgaria. The paramilitary *coup d'état* of 19 May 1934 had weakened, in some cases to the point of destroying, the role of Bulgaria's traditional political parties as well as that of the National Assembly, the country's supreme legislative body. A strong executive power was concentrated in the hands of the government, which the king, Boris III (1894–1943), appointed and controlled. A parliamentary opposition did exist nevertheless, but it was not strong. After the elections of December 1939, it comprised 19 deputies (out of 160), including 2 from the extreme right, 9 Communists or their allies, and 8 deputies from the traditional democratic parties. The regime can best be described as authoritarian, but not fascist.

And lastly, the Bulgarian Jews, numbering 48,400 according to a 1934 census, constituted eight-tenths of 1 per cent of the country's population. Ninety-seven per cent lived in the cities, about half of them in Sofia; for the most part they were workers or artisans. Although Bulgaria had its anti-Semitic traditions, they were not especially strong.

At the very beginning of the Second World War, Bulgaria chose its global strategic orientation: it would stay out of the conflict and remain neutral (no Bulgarian soldiers went to the front), while siding with its traditional ally, Germany. This stance paid off: under the provisions of the German-Soviet pact, which gave the Soviet Union the northern provinces of Rumania, on 7 September 1940 Bulgaria received southern Dobrudja (which it managed to retain at the end of the war).

It is from this moment that one can trace the development of Bulgaria's anti-Jewish policy, starting with the introduction in the legislature of the Law for the Defence of the Nation. The putative aim of this law was to prevent actions against the state, but a number of its provisions targeted the Jews specifically. Europe was in its heyday of racial legislation: the Nuremberg laws had been enacted in 1935, and now, as Boris pointed out to one of his advisers, racial measures had been imposed in Romania, Hungary, 'and even France'. It was time for Bulgaria to introduce some restrictions and regulations of her own. Starting with a definition of who exactly was a Jew, the law laid down restrictions on the right of this population to choose its place of residence, to own property, and to practise certain professions. The text of the law was drafted by

Alexander Belev, a lawyer with the ministry of internal affairs and a leading member of the Ratnik, one of Bulgaria's three main fascist organizations.

The law, first announced in October 1940 by the minister of internal affairs, Petâr Gabrovski, provoked strong reactions. Letters of protest poured into the National Assembly from professional bodies, politicians, and religious authorities, both Bulgarian Orthodox and Jewish. Others, however, expressed their patent satisfaction with the bill, notably certain business organizations and various fascist groups. Details of these reactions can be found in Dimitâr Peshev's memoirs (see pp. 137–183). The National Assembly debated the law that November and December and approved it in January 1941.

In March 1941, Bulgaria joined the Axis, the military alliance linking Germany, Italy, and Japan; Bulgaria's membership facilitated Germany's occupation of Yugoslavia and Greece. In December of that same year, when, in the wake of Japan's attack on Pearl Harbor, the United States declared war against Germany, Bulgaria did likewise against the United States and Britain. At the time, the decision had purely symbolic importance. Bulgaria assumed control of Thrace and Macedonia, first militarily, in April 1941, then administratively. 'Officially', Bulgaria had reclaimed its ancestral lands. In point of fact, however, Bulgaria did not annex these territories but only administered them; the decision as to their ultimate disposition was put off until the end of the war. Nevertheless, the presence of the Bulgarian army in the occupied territories indirectly aided the German army.

Here too, in the occupied territories the Jews were singled out. A governmental order dated 5 June 1942, concerning citizenship in 'lands liberated in 1941', decreed that 'all former Yugoslavian and Greek subjects shall become Bulgarian, unless they expressly request otherwise'. But Article 4 of the decree specified that '[This measure] does not apply to individuals of

Jewish origin, except for married Jewish women, to whom their husband's citizenship is given' (*Oceljavaneto*, p. 181). This denial of citizenship would prove fatal to the Thracian and Macedonian Jews.

The years 1941 and 1942 witnessed a slow but steady increase in anti-Jewish measures, and at the same time a worsening of Jewish living conditions. The Jewish community tried to organize a number of sailings to Palestine, but with catastrophic results: the first ship to leave, the *Salvator*, sank in the Sea of Marmara on 12 December 1940 with 180 people on board; the second, the *Struma*, which set sail from Romania, sank with 400 passengers and crew. The ships were old and in poor condition. Various efforts to arrange the legal departure for Palestine of a certain number of Jews failed. Moreover, the British authorities responsible for administering the Palestine Protectorate were in no great hurry to receive boatloads of refugees. A few months later, referring to the Bulgarian Jews' requests for entry visas into Palestine, Anthony Eden, the British Foreign Minister, replied, 'Were we to undertake such steps, Jews the world over will ask us to do the same in Poland and in Germany. Hitler might very well take us at our word' (Boyadjieff, p. 73).

In the meantime, the Bulgarian government had imposed a curfew on the Jews, curtailed their freedoms, evicted some from their homes, or forcibly conscripted them into special work gangs; they were also required to wear the yellow Star of David. Nevertheless, the administration took considerable liberties in applying these orders; the king and his ministers alike maintained cordial relations with prominent members of the Jewish community, and Bulgarian consulates abroad continued to issue visas to Jews who requested them. The section in charge of Jewish questions within the German foreign office in Berlin was beginning to grow impatient.

The course of events took a precipitous turn in the autumn

of 1942. Towards the end of August, a new decree was issued, outlining a series of additional measures regulating the public life of the Jews and creating a Commissariat for Jewish Questions, attached to the ministry of internal affairs. Belev was appointed to oversee its operations. The German ambassador to Sofia, Adolf Beckerle, and his police (Gestapo) attaché, Karl Hoffman, received assurances from Prime Minister Bogdan Filov and Minister of Internal Affairs Gabrovski that the deportation of the Jews could begin at any time. Yet for the moment, the Bulgarian leaders insisted, the Jews were needed for various tasks inside Bulgaria, particularly road maintenance.

On 21 January 1943, the deportation of the Bulgarian Jews entered its critical phase, with the arrival in Sofia of Theodor Dannecker, SS Hauptsturmführer and Eichmann's special envoy. Having first determined the number of Jews to be deported – 20,000 – Dannecker presented his demand to Belev, his Bulgarian counterpart. Together they decided on how that number was to be divided: 14,000 Jews, they estimated, could be deported from the occupied territories (8000 from Macedonia and 6000 from Thrace); the remaining 6000 were to be taken from 'old' Bulgaria – that is, from within the country's pre-1940 boundaries. Dannecker suggested that they begin with Jewish 'undesirables'.

During the first days of February, Belev issued instructions to the Commissariat's delegates in the new territories to prepare for the impending operations. They must not arouse suspicion or reveal the transports' true destination. At first, only men were to be arrested, then their families would be instructed to join them. 'The women will be told that they are being taken to join their husbands, so that the reunited families can be settled in old Bulgaria' *(Oceljavaneto,* p. 207). On 12 February the cabinet, apparently after lengthy debate, approved Belev's proposals, including those specifying the

7

number of Jews to be arrested. In a communication of 16 February to the Reich's security office, Dannecker reported with satisfaction that preparations for the deportation were under way and that it would begin in early March.

On 22 February, Dannecker and Belev signed an accord concerning the impending deportation. It was formally agreed that 20,000 persons were to be deported, without regard to age or sex; also decided was which stations the Jews would leave from, and on which trains. The accord included cost-sharing arrangements (the Bulgarian railroads would pay for transport to the border, but not beyond), and specified that the Bulgarian government would renounce any future jurisdictional claims over its subjects (which in fact they would no longer be): 'In those cases where the Jews being deported are not yet deprived of their citizenship, this must occur at their departure from Bulgarian territory' (*Oceljavaneto*, p. 205). The same day, the Commissariat circulated a memorandum to its local delegates requesting that within the following twenty-four hours they each draw up a list of 'rich, prominent, and generally well-known' Jews, as well as community leaders and opponents of the regime (*Oceljavaneto*, p. 206). On 2 March 1943 the cabinet formalized the earlier instructions, and the machinery was set in motion.

The deportations went according to plan. Beginning on 4 March, the Thracian Jews were arrested and transferred to 'old Bulgaria'; by 11 March, the internment of Jews from Macedonia and the town of Pirot, on the Serbian border, had also been completed. Ambassador Beckerle could thus note in his diary on 3 March that 'Dannecker informed me that as of yesterday the round-up of the Thracian Jews had begun, and that the Macedonian Jews had already been resettled in the ghetto; only girls less than fourteen years of age are permitted to leave [the ghetto] to buy food and other necessities' (*Oceljavaneto* p. 210). On 18 and 19 March, the Thracian Jews were taken by train to Lom, a Danube river port, where they boarded barges bound for Vienna; from there, they were transferred by train to Katowice and Auschwitz. The Macedonia Jews were transferred by train directly to Auschwitz, on 22 and 25 March, and to Treblinka on 29 March. In all, 11,343 people were deported. Twelve of them would survive.

The detention and deportation did not go unnoticed in 'old Bulgaria', where the Jewish deportees were several days in transit; eyewitnesses reacted with compassion and outrage, numerous traces of which remain – Dimitâr Ikonomov's account to his colleague Peshev (see p. 158), which helped spur the latter to action; statements made by Stefan, metropolitan of Sofia (the Orthodox equivalent of an archbishop) (p. 99); the demand by Petko Stainov, an opposition member of the National Assembly, to the prime minister (p. 81). Stefan, in particular, wasted no time in alerting the king, pleading with him by telegram to spare the Thracian Jews, whose transport train he had encountered as it crossed Bulgaria. But as Stefan himself said even at the time, his entreaties fell on deaf ears.

For the Jews of 'old Bulgaria', events took a different turn. Their arrests began on 3 March in various provincial cities and were carried out according to lists drawn up by the Commissariat. Unlike their Thracian and Macedonian brothers, however, they could count on support from their Bulgarian friends. The clearest example of this comes from the town of Kyustendil, not far from Sofia. There the arrests, aimed at a local Jewish population of about one thousand, began on 7 March. On 8 March, a delegation of forty people decided to go to Sofia to plead the case of their fellow citizens. In the end, only four of them went: a lawyer, a retired professor, a businessman (Asen Suichmezov), and the local deputy to the National Assembly, Petâr Mikhalev; none of these men was Jewish. Arriving at night in Sofia, they made an appointment for the next day with another deputy from Kyustendil, Dimitâr Peshev, who was also vice-chairman of the National Assembly. As his memoirs make clear, Peshev had already been informed of what was happening; he invited the visitors to meet him at the National Assembly that same afternoon. He demanded to speak with Prime Minister Filov; this, he was told, was impossible, but he and a delegation of seven other deputies would be received by Minister of Internal Affairs Gabrovski. At first, Gabrovski disavowed any knowledge of the arrests; ultimately, at the insistence of his visitors, who refused to leave, he picked up the telephone and ordered that the arrests cease and that those who had been arrested be released.

The same scenario was repeated in other provincial cities (but with somewhat lesser degrees of success). Later, we shall read an eyewitness account of Cyril, metropolitan of Plovdiv and future patriarch of Bulgaria: he sent his own telegram to the king, interceded with the administrative authorities, and allowed Jews to take refuge in his house; it is said of Cyril that he vowed to lie across the rails in the path of the first train transport of Jews from his diocese. In Sofia, numerous public figures intervened with their relatives and friends in government circles.

Peshev, who had already played a critical role in this reversal of the government's plans, decided to push his advantage even further. He quickly composed a letter of protest which was signed by forty-two other representatives of the majority party and sent it to the chairman of the Assembly (see p. 78). In measured terms, this statement condemned the government's anti-Jewish policy and demanded it be changed. Filov, once he learned of the statement, was angered at this challenge to his authority. Seeking to humiliate Peshev personally, he demanded, during a meeting of his party's deputies, that all those who had signed the protest letter withdraw their support. To his disappointment, thirty deputies refused to comply. Filov also called for a vote of censure against Peshev and had him stripped of his duties as Assembly vice-chairman. At no time was Peshev given the chance to defend himself publicly. Nevertheless, the plans for deporting the Bulgarian Jews had been abandoned for the time being.

So ended the final episode of the Jewish deportation; the operation had been completely successful in Thrace and Macedonia but had totally failed in Bulgaria proper. Officials from the German legation did not appear terribly disappointed. 'Under these circumstances,' they wrote on 5 April 1943, 'the actual outcome, 11,343 Jews deported, must be considered satisfactory. Fifty-six per cent of our target of 20,000 was achieved' (*Oceljavaneto*, p. 237).

Dannecker and Belev did not abandon the idea of deporting the totality of Bulgaria's Jewish population; Eichmann's office continued to stress the importance of this imperative. Acting in concert, the two men put pressure on Filov and Gabrovski, who assured them of their good intentions. From the other side, Jewish organizations, religious authorities, and various political figures tried to convince those in positions of power, especially the king, that all plans for the deportation must be halted. Seizing on a few acts of resistance in which Jews had taken part, Belev in early May 1943 drafted a new plan, with the following alternative: 'Plan A: the deportation of all Bulgarian Jews to Germany's eastern regions for reasons of internal state security; Plan B: the evacuation of Sofia's 25,000 Jews to the provinces, should the preceding plan prove unfeasible.' Gabrovski agreed to Plan A and submitted it to Boris at an audience with the king on 20 May 1943. 'The king,' Hoffmann wrote in his 7 June report, 'decided that evacuation of the Jews to the provinces should begin at once. For this reason, Plan A has been abandoned' (*Oceljavaneto*, p. 257). On 21 May, the cabinet ratified the king's decision. The international situation, after Stalingrad and the Allied victories in North Africa, had begun to change, as had public opinion within Bulgaria itself; henceforth the king would categorically oppose deportation as such.

Sofia's Jewish population greeted the news of their impending evacuation and internment with panic and depression. Protests multiplied, with the Bulgarian Orthodox Church and a number of prominent citizens at the forefront of the opposition. Metropolitan Stefan, who was extremely active during this period, sent Boris a telegram that read as follows: 'Do not judge, so that you may not be judged. For with the judgment you make you will be judged, and the measure you give will be the measure you get [Matthew 7:1–2]. Know, Boris, that God watches your actions from Heaven' (*Oceljava-neto*, p. 42). Stefan also received Bulgaria's Chief Rabbi at his home. The traditional Cyril and Methodius' Day parade on 24 May (Cyril and Methodius' Day is a Bulgarian national holiday in honour of culture and education) turned into a mass demonstration against the government's anti-Jewish policies; some 400 people were arrested. Nonetheless, the evacuation of Sofia's Jews to the provinces went ahead and continued through the month of June; nearly 20,000 Jews were forced to leave the capital. Yet deportation to the concentration camps of Poland had still not occurred.

Had it merely been postponed? Dannecker and Belev hoped so, but few seemed to share their hopes. In his 7 June report, ambassador Beckerle had already expressed a different view of the situation. First, he cast Belev as an opponent of the government's policies and said that he could not be trusted. Belev, wrote Beckerle, had adopted the official position of Bulgaria's rulers, which boiled down to the following: 'Of course we agree, in principle, to resolve the "Jewish question"; but as a practical matter, we need our Jews for the time being (they are building roads!); besides, their deportation would come at too high a political price, both internally and internationally.'

The Allies had landed in Sicily, and Bulgaria wanted more than ever to preserve its neutrality (anti-Soviet propaganda was forbidden in Bulgaria, particularly if it was directed against Stalin). In a subsequent report, dated 18 August 1943, Beckerle arrived at the following conclusion: 'I have realized, in my conversations with the said ministers and in my meeting yesterday with the prime minister, that to insist on the deportation at the present time makes no sense whatsoever.' He had not abandoned all hope, but qualified it heavily: 'When Germany's [military] success becomes apparent and the political offensive against us recedes, that will be the time for us to act' (*Oceljavaneto*, pp. 264–5). Only German military victory could have allowed the deportations to resume.

On 28 August, a few days after his final visit to Hitler, Boris died suddenly. As Crown Prince Simeon was still a minor, three regents were appointed, Filov being one of them. A new government was formed, and at the beginning of October Belev was replaced by another commissar, someone not particularly known for his anti-Semitism. By the end of the month, Sofia's Jews had been granted permission to return to their homes, and over the course of the following year various anti-Jewish measures were abolished; on 31 August 1944, on the eve of Bulgaria's occupation by the Soviet army, the cabinet rescinded the Law for the Defence of the Nation. On 9 September 1944, the old regime collapsed.

Memories in Competition

The rescue of the Bulgarian Jews, even if partial (since the Thracian and Macedonian Jews were in fact deported), was undeniably a meritorious act. The question is, who merits credit for it?

The Communist regime that gradually took power in Bulgaria after 9 September 1944 gave two mutually contradictory answers to that question: first, what happened was not all that important; and, second, the Communist Party deserves all credit for this glorious achievement.

What happened was not all that important: this is the conclusion one might well have drawn had one been following the proceedings of the People's Tribunal, the court of exceptional jurisdiction responsible for the 1944 purges. For, having decided to put all deputies from the government majority on trial for having supported the policies of the previous government, the Tribunal chose not to take into much account their actions at the time of the Jewish deportation. Of the forty-three delegates who had signed Peshev's protest letter, twenty were sentenced to death, six to life imprisonment, eight (including Peshev himself) to fifteen-year prison terms, four others to five-year terms, and one to a prison term of a year; three were acquitted and another died while awaiting sentencing (Nissim, pp. 225-6, 315-16). Among the most notable of those executed were Ikonomov, who had been the first to sound the alarm, and Ivan Petrov,

14

who had fought hard in the National Assembly against the Law for the Defence of the Nation; Mikhalev, at Peshev's side throughout his efforts, received a life sentence. Those sentenced to imprisonment eventually saw their prison terms reduced. Metropolitan Stefan was relieved of his responsibilities.

The judicial apparatus, now in the hands of the Communists, was not alone in treating the actions of Peshev and his colleagues as insignificant. Important liberal opposition figures, such as Petko Stainov, a National Assembly delegate, and the journalist Dimo Kazasov, who had stood up courageously against the deportation, now held positions of power: Stainov was minister of foreign affairs and Kazasov minister of information. Recognizing the merits of their political adversaries clearly did not rank among their first concerns. Even though Stainov testified at Peshev's trial, he did not speak in his defence.

Nor were all members of Bulgaria's Jewish community eager to express their gratitude to these fallen public figures. When it was time to find a lawyer for Peshev, who as vice-chairman of the National Assembly was a particular target of accusations, his family turned initially to a prominent Communist and Jewish lawyer, Nissim Mevorakh. He refused to take the case, citing 'political reasons'. Peshev's court-appointed attorney, David Ligi, failed to show up on the first day of the hearings, producing a medical certificate to justify his absence. The former victims of persecution, now that they were out of danger, did not necessarily take up the fight against this new persecution. But not everyone made the same choice. Yosif Yasharov, another lawyer of Jewish extraction, agreed to defend Peshev and actually saved his life by proving mitigating circumstances. Ironically, it was not what Peshev had done to save the Jews that swayed the court, but rather something he had done years earlier, in 1936, when, as minister of justice in a previous administration, he had blocked the execution of an opposition figure who now, in the wake of the Communist takeover of 9 September, was minister of defence. Peshev's 1936 action had cost him his post in a subsequent cabinet reshuffling. As for Yasharov, he would pay dearly for saving Peshev's life: in 1948, he was disbarred, the Sofia bar association citing his 'reactionary tendencies' as the reason for his expulsion (Nissim, pp. 210–22).

Long after the 1944 trials, the Jewish genocide was still not recognized as such in Bulgaria. A 1954 textbook, for example, devotes a single sentence to it: 'Imitating the Hitlerites, the government had the National Assembly pass a Law for the Defence of the Nation, which targeted Bulgaria's Jews.' Apparently, neither the deportation of the Macedonian and Thracian Jews nor the failed deportation of the Bulgarian Jews was deemed worthy of mention. According to the official Bulgarian encyclopaedia, the concentration camps held only political prisoners; in Auschwitz, the encyclopaedia goes on to say, 'prisoners of all nationalities' were killed.

Such was the original Communist view of the Jewish persecution during the war. Another, entirely different version existed as well, according to which the persecution was indeed one of the great crimes of the preceding regime, which had failed thanks to the heroic actions of the Communist Party. This new version was formulated and put forth by a number of Jewish Communists, the first to collect and publish documentary evidence concerning these events. After the mass exodus of Bulgarian Jews to Israel, in 1948 and 1949, all publications connected with the Jewish community wound up in the hands of ardent Communists. The *Annals* (*Godishnik*) of the Social, Cultural, and Educational Organization of the Jews in Bulgaria, which first appeared in 1966 and which pursued the publication of wartime documents relating to the Jewish community, held firm to this line.

The Communist Party downplayed the events of March 1943, in which it had no role at all, emphasizing instead those of May 1943, especially the 24 May demonstration against the evacuation and internment measures. This demonstration, in the party's telling of it, had been organized and led by representatives of the Workers' Party (the name under which the Communist Party, illegal since 1925, had operated). After 1954, when power passed into the hands of Todor Jivkov (Bulgaria's president until 1989, when he was forced out of office), people began to 'realize' that it was none other than Jivkov who had spearheaded this glorious action. Praise for Jivkov would grow ever more extravagant with passing years, until, towards the end of the 1970s, the organization found itself pressured into nominating Jivkov for the Nobel Peace Prize for his role in the rescue of the Bulgarian Jews; ultimately, nothing came of the nomination (Nissim, p. 264).

To what extent are these claims legitimate?

Let us say first of all that during the war the Communists did in fact oppose the persecution of the Jews in all its forms. It is true that they sought to make use of this cause, harnessing it to their overall political objectives, which were to overthrow the existing power structure and be regarded as the most active combatants in the fight against fascism; this, of course, is the kind of thing politicians are supposed to do. There is ample evidence of the party's efforts to fight anti-Semitism in its deputies' speeches in the National Assembly, dating, that is, from the days when they could still speak their hearts and minds (after the Soviet invasion, these legislators would be suspended and imprisoned). This evidence is also to be found in the political tracts and clandestine newspapers that the party distributed and in its radio broadcasts from Soviet territory (see pp. 65, 73, 75, and 108). But did these interventions play as important a role as Communist historians would have it? That is what remains to be determined.

Frankly, nothing points in this direction. The protests of the Communist deputies when the Law for the Defence of the Nation was still a draft bill were generally taken as a propaganda ploy, which in fact was what they were, among other things; and, in any case, the protests of this or that deputy were to absolutely no avail: a compliant government majority passed the bill in January 1941. At the time of the deportation itself, in March 1943, the Communists were in no position to stand in the way of the operation, which continued. The party, which at that time was banned and subject to government repression, had little influence; had the Jews been perceived as being close to the Communists, they would have suffered even greater persecution. Finally, the 24 May parade was organized primarily by leaders of the Jewish community, notably Rabbi Daniel Tsion. As for Jivkov, he seems to have played no role in it whatsoever; in the *Oceljavaneto* anthology, published in Sofia in 1995 but still apologetic with regard to the Communists, the editors drily note that 'The version of T. Jivkov, former secretary of the Third Regional Committee of the Bulgarian Workers' Party, that the Central Committee assigned him the task of organizing and leading the demonstration . . . was not confirmed by research studies.'

If it was not the Communists who saved the Bulgarian Jews, then who did? In the early 1950s, a second thesis emerged, diametrically opposed to the first. According to this thesis, the true saviour of the Jews was none other than Boris III. This thesis was first put forward in the Bulgarian émigré press, notably in 1952 by Benjamin Arditi, a Bulgarian Jew who had emigrated to Israel. It was taken up again and again in Bulgarian expatriate newspapers, but also, after 1990, in Bulgaria itself. It had two obvious advantages: it deprived the Communists of any credit for the rescue, and it ascribed a noble role to their historical enemy, the king. Also, for some people, there must have been something reassuring in this fairy-tale ending: the king was good and wise after all.

But if one turns to the historical documents, the first thing one notices is that it is impossible to take the king's words at face value. When Boris spoke (he did not write frequently), it was not to reveal his inner thoughts nor to put into words the world he saw around him; he spoke in order to act on those he addressed, so that they would do what he wanted them to do. To each of them the king had different things to say, and everything he said was intended to serve his chosen ends. To the Jews seeking his protection he promised that nothing would happen to them; to the Germans demanding the Jews' deportation, he answered that there was nothing he wanted more. To his various confidants, ministers, and advisers, he never gave the same answer twice. Therefore, the only way to judge the king's attitude toward the Jews is to probe his actions, not his words.

From 10 March 1943 until his death on 28 August of that year, the king held firm to the position that the Jews were not to be deported. Peshev and his fellow deputies' action could not have stopped the deportation, had Boris, who held supreme power in Bulgaria, wanted it carried out. Contemporary documents confirm this. In his dispatch of 5 April 1943, Hoffmann writes that 'it appears that the minister of internal affairs has received from the highest levels [*von höchster Stelle*] an order to stop the planned transfer of the Jews from old Bulgaria' (*Oceljavanto*, p. 236; German text in Boyadjieff, p. 79). The wording is revealing: the German functionaries present this information as a deduction, not as an empirical fact, and they avoid naming the king personally. Nevertheless, in the Bulgaria of 1943 'the highest levels' can refer to one and only one person. On 9 March, Gabrovski agreed to suspend his orders, believing that he could proceed with them the following day; it must have been a subsequent action by the king – though no evidence of it remains – that prevented him from doing so. During the next attempt at deportation, in May 1943, Boris intervened once again: as we have seen, in an audience with his minister of internal affairs on 20 May, the king, rejecting the latter's advice, deferred the deportation and opted for evacuation instead. In the face of German pressure, he hedged: yes, he would be very pleased if the Germans resolved his 'Jewish question', but for the moment he really needs 'his' Jews for road maintenance. It is no surprise that Goebbels describes him in his diary as being 'cunning like a fox'.

Be that as it may, the king was in fact responsible for the deportation to the death camps of 11,343 people from the occupied territories of Thrace and Macedonia. Of course these people were not Bulgarian citizens, but it was his government that, in its decree of 5 June 1942, had taken away their citizenship. Boris did not initiate the deportation (it was the responsibility of Dannecker and Belev), but he did nothing to stop it, even though he had the means to do so. He clearly knew what was happening and he also knew what fate awaited the Jewish deportees. And if he did not know, all he had to do was listen to people who had witnessed the operations. The Swiss chargé d'affaires, Charles Rédard, met with Filov on 11 March 1943 and pleaded with him to stop the deportation, making it quite clear that the Jews being sent to Poland faced certain death (see p. 92); it is highly unlikely that Filov kept this information to himself and did not share it with the king. The testimony of Stefan, the metropolitan of Sofia, is particularly devastating. Having witnessed the Jewish suffering at first hand, he sent Boris a telegram begging him to stop the deportation. 'In answer to our telegram, we received a message informing us that everything possible and legal would be done' (see p. 126). In other words, the operation would proceed, because it was being carried out in strict accordance with the law.

On his return to Sofia, Stefan again wrote to the palace. 'My efforts came to naught,' he wrote on 2 April 1943; 'shortly afterwards, the deportees were transported to the Danube ports' (p. 100). Refusing to give up, he sent a report to the king. The palace official who received it let Stefan know that the king 'had responded favourably to our first appeal, ordering that the Jews exiled from Thrace be well treated in crossing Bulgaria, even though they were prisoners of Hitler's high military command' (p. 130). Did the Bulgarian police officers who accompanied the transports receive these orders? Whether they did or not, the fate of the deportees remained the same, while Bulgarian consciences were cheaply assuaged. This refusal on the part of the king to heed the religious authorities was unusual enough to prompt Stefan to note in his memoirs that 'this was the only time, in all our frequent professional contacts with the King, that we encountered silence and aloofness' (p. 131).

Stefan was not alone in his efforts; deputies from the government majority (such as Ikonomov) as well as opposition deputies (Stainov) protested publicly. Other metropolitans who had witnessed the deportations spoke out as well. 'In Skopje [Macedonia],' wrote Sofroni, 'they arrested all the Jews – men, women, children, the infirm. They were brought together to a large tobacco warehouse, where they were held under strict guard. Later they were sent to Poland' (*Oceljava-neto*, p. 232). Neither the government nor the king could have been unaware of these appeals. Nevertheless, they went unanswered.

On 31 March 1943, Boris paid a visit to Hitler at his residence in Berchtesgaden and on the following day had long conversations with his host and with Joachim von Ribbentrop, Hitler's foreign minister. The recent deportations were not far from his thoughts. Here, in Filov's words, are Boris's impressions of the meeting: '[The king] discussed the Jewish question with Ribbentrop at length, trying to explain to him that Bulgaria's Jews are Spanish [i.e., Sephardim], and that they in no way play the role they do in other countries. But it seems that Ribbentrop didn't accept these objections and replied that a Jew is always a Jew' (Filov's diary entry of 5 April 1943; see p. 89).

Ribbentrop, in a telegram to Beckerle, gives a somewhat different account of this conversation. 'As far as the Jewish question in Bulgaria is concerned,' he writes, 'the king says that for the time being, he only agreed to transfer Jews from Macedonia and Thrace to Eastern Europe [i.e., Poland]. As far as Bulgaria's Jews are concerned, he only wants to get rid of an insignificant number – the Bolshevik-Communist elements; he wants to hold onto the 25,000 Jews now in concentration centres; he says he wants to use them for road construction. I let these comments pass, and simply stressed that, in our view, the only appropriate solution to the Jewish question is the radical one' (4 April 1943, *Oceljavaneto*, p. 234).

The differences between the two versions are telling. Boris presents himself to Filov as a great supporter of the Jews, despite the fact that Filov supported the deportations (but you never know). But with Ribbentrop, Boris stresses that he had authorized the deportation of the Thracian and Macedonian Jews, and then he promises to expel some Bulgarian Jews as well, provided they are pro-Communists. But how many of them? If one subtracts the 25,000 Jews that Boris wished to retain from the total of 48,000 that the Nazis were demanding, that leaves some 23,000 candidates for deportation. Did the king ever intend to keep his word, or was he merely trying to placate his German interlocutor with vague assurances? In the end, Boris proposed keeping the remaining Jews in concentration centres. Another dodge? Undoubtedly. In any case, the difference between such measures and 'the radical solution' is strikingly obvious.

In the light of these documents and personal accounts, Boris appears to have played a less heroic role than his admirers ascribe to him. His actions were guided by self-interest, or rather, by what he saw as Bulgaria's interests; for someone like Boris, who identified completely with his country, the two were indistinguishable. What motivated him was national interest as he understood it, not humanitarian principles. Small countries have to come to terms with great ones. Hitler had the power; thus some of his demands had to be accepted. The king did manage to keep Bulgaria's soldiers out of the fray (the army's occupation of the promised lands of Thrace and Macedonia notwithstanding). But when it came to turning over the Jews, as Hitler, Himmler, and Ribbentrop demanded, it was necessary to yield somewhat here in order to gain elsewhere; in other words, to deport the Jews from the occupied territories but not those from 'old Bulgaria'; to expel the Jews from Sofia but not from Bulgaria. This in fact was how Beckerle tried to cast the events, at his own trial in 1968: the king, he said, had agreed to the deportation of the Thracian and Macedonian Jews, but had secretly asked for his cooperation, so that the deportation of Jews from old Bulgaria might be derailed (Boyadjieff, p. 72). Boris's policy was a calculated move, designed to make shift with the powerful of this world. It managed to save some lives – four-fifths of Bulgaria's Jewish population – at the expense of the remainder.

Was it for humanitarian reasons that the king chose to stand behind Bulgaria's Jews? On the contrary, everything suggests that, here again, Boris's choice was a political one. During that spring of 1943, Hitler's victory was not the foregone conclusion it had once appeared to be. Boris did not want to compromise Bulgaria's relations with the United States and Great Britain, which had made plain to him their firm opposition to the Nazis' anti-Jewish policies. Nor could he entirely ignore the changing tide of public opinion at home. There had been public protests when the Law for the Defence of the Nation was being voted on, just as there would be later, in May 1943, during the evacuation; Boris had demonstrated his capacity for indifference. Why did he change his behaviour subsequent to March 1943? Because of Peshev's intervention in the National Assembly, a first: this action, a virtual insurrection within the government majority, showed that a third of its members were ready to repudiate the government on the Jewish question. Taking into account this new balance of power, the king decided henceforth to oppose the deportation of the Bulgarian Jews.

Had the king not made that choice, the Jews might well have been deported; but had Peshev and his like-minded colleagues not acted as they did, the king would probably have decided differently. And so we come to a third way of responding to our initial question as to the rightful credit for the rescue, which is to put the emphasis on Peshev's action. Italian journalist and historian Gabriele Nissim, like certain other witnesses to the drama, does precisely this in a recent biography of Peshev. Nissim stresses the exceptional nature of Peshev's action in the 1943 European context; he may not have been the only person to have helped the Jews, but he is the only one to have led a legal, parliamentary action in their defence; he fought not for one or two individuals but for all of them together.

In point of fact, Peshev did not stand alone in Bulgaria. The letters of protest, the telephone calls, the personal steps taken at the time of the Assembly debates and during the round-ups: none of these measures would have been enough, taken individually, to stop the machinery of oppression. But quantity became quality, and by their number these actions changed the general atmosphere: persecution lost its sheen of victory. The declared (p. 92); everyone has dark forebodings concerning their fate, Peshev was told by fellow deputy Ikonomov (p. 158); the protest letter that Peshev wrote and forty-two other deputies signed referred to 'cruel measures … that may expose the government and the entire nation to accusations of mass murder' (p. 80). This is what any well-meaning person living in a European country in 1943 could have known. But when we know that evil is striking our neighbour, the question is, do we do anything about it? And if so, why? And how?

The king, who held supreme power in Bulgaria, acted, as I said earlier, on the basis of national interest. From the moment he judged that the deportation of the Jews would harm his country's reputation and hence compromise its future, he opposed it determinedly and effectively. He may have been confirmed in his decision by the appeals for compassion made by various moral and religious authorities. This union of self-interest and virtue is a particularly solid one. Unfortunately, it seldom happens. In March 1943, the king apparently did not feel that saving the lives of Jews was in his country's vital interest; accordingly, he authorized the deportation of the first 11,343. As the ultimate grounds for action, national interest does not by itself offer firm terrain; it substitutes 'what is good for us' for what is good as such.

Those who lacked decision-making powers but who nevertheless participated in public life acted – that is, when they did act – in the name of some law. Sometimes, this law was a written law; the Union of Lawyers, for example, like the opposition deputies, pointed to an article in the Constitution, which held that all individuals are equal before the law. The Church leadership, in one of its reports, spoke of 'the word of our Saviour in whose eyes all are children of one heavenly Father' (p. 55). Others may not have been able to cite any particular law but spoke of the suffering of the victims: they acted out of humanity. It was impossible for them to remain

intercessions with the king, even those that on the face of it seemed futile, still counted. Appeals to the good sense of the Assembly deputies, though ignored then and there, acted quietly nevertheless on their hearts and minds.

Among these various appeals, those of the Bulgarian Orthodox Church were particularly important, and as the situation worsened, the Church's stance grew firmer and firmer. At the time of the first Assembly debates on the Law for the Defence of the Nation, the metropolitans were stressing the difference between converted or baptized Jews who had adopted the Christian faith, and the rest, demanding, above all, full protection for the former. At the same time, the clerics asked that the latter, the non-converted, be judged by what they did, not for who they were (see p. 56). During one meeting of the Synod, on 2 April 1943, even those who had defended the law now attacked its implementation. Yosif, metropolitan of Varna, for example, said, 'Toward the non-Christian Jews, our relations must be those of universal morality, of one man to another' (*Oceljavaneto*, p. 231). Another metropolitan, Kliment of Stara Zagora, added that, in acting as they did, the government bodies were behaving like Communists, not like Christians. Cyril of Plovdiv and, above all, Stefan were particularly outspoken. Stefan fired off one report after another; the king was unmoved, while the prime minister threatened to haul Stefan into court for actions hostile to the state (see p. 131). Stefan responded by announcing that the doors of every Bulgarian church and monastery would be opened to the Jews.

Peshev, then, if he is to be properly understood, must be situated among these various other actors. The difference between him and them lay primarily in his greater efficacy. This lawyer, born in 1894, served as minister of justice from 1935 to 1936; then, in 1939, he became a deputy in the National Assembly for the conservative, majority party and the

Assembly's vice-chairman. He did not oppose the Law for the Defence of the Nation while it was being debated in the Assembly, and, as we shall see, even thirty years later, while writing his memoirs, he could not completely dismiss the arguments that had led to its adoption. He lost his post after his action in March 1943 but not his seat in the Assembly; arrested in late 1944 by Bulgaria's new Communist rulers, he was convicted of the charges brought against him and sentenced to prison, but was released at the end of 1945. He spent the rest of his life, until his death in 1973, in a kind of internal exile, rarely leaving his room. From 1969 to 1970, he wrote his invaluable memoirs, in which he sets out in great detail his opinions and his recollections concerning all the questions of public life that faced him over the years, including the persecution of the Jews (see p. 137). His memoirs contain a vigorous and, within the context of Communist Bulgaria, stinging defence of democracy, parliamentary principles, and personal freedoms. Peshev is one of the thirteen 'righteous' Bulgarians officially honoured by the State of Israel.

Memories conflict because the glorious role in the past – the role of the hero or, in other contexts, of the victim – constitutes a precious symbolic capital in the present, one that confers prestige, legitimacy, and, ultimately, more power on those who can successfully lay claim to it. But memory is not merely a place where wills collide, each seeking advantage over the others. Memory is also open to the establishment of truth. It is either true or false that the Communists were responsible for the rescue of the Jews; it is either true or false that Boris did his best to spare all of Bulgaria's Jews from deportation. If memory is to become history, the battle of opposing wills to power needs to recede into the background and leave room for the search for truth: an endless search perhaps, but necessary nonetheless.

Why and How

The past requires not only that we study it and know it, but also that we learn its lessons – for this simple reason: evil is not just a thing of the past. The rescue of the Bulgarian Jews is one of the rare bright pages in the history of the Jews in those dark times; it was also and irrefutably a positive political act, which, by its rarity, deserves our full attention. For if we understand better its circumstances and the motivations of those responsible for it, perhaps we will be better able ourselves to act tomorrow.

In March 1943, Prime Minister Filov seems to have been the only person in Bulgaria who thought that the Jews would not be worse off for being deported. Everyone else knew otherwise, whether they took satisfaction in the situation or saw it as a source of shame. Accurate information was scarce, the details of the extermination were still obscure, and often what passed for news at the time we know today to have been false rumour (for example, execution by electrocution). Nonetheless, one had only to see how Jewish families – children and old people included – were being arrested, treated, and transported: one had only to listen to what was being said by spokesmen for the Allies or by representatives from neutral countries like Switzerland, to realize that German references to pressing needs for manual labour were thinly disguised fictions that no one really believed. 'They are being sent to their death,' Charles Rédard, the Swiss chargé d'affaires

indifferent and passive in the face of the pain that the actions of men had brought into the world. 'People have described terrifying and heart-rending scenes and told me of the horrible conditions under which the Jews are being held,' wrote Stefan at the time of these events. '[They] were being treated with inhuman cruelty' (p. 100). It is important to remember that all this was taking place then and there on Bulgarian soil, and those who 'treated' the Jews in this way were Bulgarian police and state employees. Ikonomov, in his appeal to Peshev, describes similar reactions in the onlookers, speaking of 'their anger and outrage, their inability to remain indifferent to the tragedy that was unfolding before their eyes: this multitude of women and children and old people who were being taken who knows where' (p. 158).

What motivated these individuals who, when the time came, dared to say no? Peshev's memoirs shed some light on this subject. One should remember, first of all, that in the autumn of 1940, Peshev saw no reason not to adopt the Law for the Defence of the Nation, and he voted in favour of it. His argument was one of national interest: concessions had to be made towards the Germans, since Bulgaria depended on them and isolating the Jews seemed to keep the Germans happy; besides, the law would not be enforced and no one would really be bothered. If he began to change his mind during the first months of 1943, it was because where once he had seen abstractions – rules, laws, regulations, Jews – he now saw individual faces, and they were faces of people who were suffering.

First, there was the account given him by Ikonomov, who, as Peshev rightly points out, was something of a political adversary. Therefore, if they came together, it was not out of strategic or tactical considerations but because they both were 'decent' men (p. 158), ready to act according to their

29

convictions rather than their immediate interests. That Ikonomov had decided to approach him, his long-time adversary,
was for Peshev an indication that the other's reaction was
authentic. Ikonomov's account speaks not in abstractions or
principles but of the plight of individuals: 'Thracian Jews, old
people, men, women and children, carrying their belongings,
defeated, desperate, powerless people, begging for help as they
crossed the town on foot, dragging themselves towards some
unknown destination' (p. 158). The sacrifice borne by the
Thracian Jews would thus serve to save their brothers, because
it would rouse the conscience of Bulgaria's legislators and high
clergy.

A few days later, Peshev learned of plans for a new round-
up, this time in the town of Kyustendil, his electoral district. It
was then that he made his decision. 'I could not remain passive
– my conscience and understanding ... did not allow it' (p.
159). As Peshev describes this moment, it was as though his
will had been overcome by a superior force. He no longer had
a choice, and he had to act now. The deportation had been
ordered by the government but it violated both written and
unwritten laws. 'That agreement ... in violation of the
Constitution, the ordinary rule of law, common decency and
basic human sympathy, could not be implemented and, from a
legal standpoint, was null and void' (p. 163). From that
moment forward, action was necessary, silence intolerable,
civil disobedience a duty. 'To remain silent would have been a
breach of conscience, it would have been contrary to my sense
of responsibility both as a deputy and as a human being ...
Inaction by the majority on this question would have made it
complicit not only to ... a violation of the Constitution, but to
much more – to criminal felony plain and simple: the mass
murder of thousands of human beings' (pp. 163–4). How
many political leaders in 1943 could honestly say they had
spoken and acted thus?

Besides the powerful and the visible, there was also the great mass of the population, who did not participate directly in political life yet whose actions clearly counted. It would be an exaggeration, of course, to imagine that there was no anti-Semitism among the Bulgarian people. The existence of militant right-wing organizations like the Ratnik, the Brannik or the Legionnaires reminds us otherwise, as do high-profile activists like Belev, as well as anti-Semites of the garden variety, like the man who attacked Asen Suichmezov, a defender of Jews. 'Popov, the waiter, was very hostile to Jews. As soon as he saw me, he grabbed a chair and tried to smash me over the head with it' (p. 133). Even those who defended the Jews often reveal what looks like a kind of acceptance of the discrimination to which the latter had been subject. Stainov, for example, in a speech to the National Assembly, assures his colleagues that 'Jews have never participated in Bulgaria's political or public life. There are no Jews in the Assembly ... Nor are there any in the officer corps, in the theatre, in the press corps, in the telegraph agencies, insofar as we have any, nor in the diplomatic corps or the civil service' (p. 63). And all this, of course, was true. Nevertheless, it would be incorrect to say that the majority of the Bulgarian people harboured anti-Semitic feelings, and this lack of animosity on their part contributed unquestionably to the rescue of the Jews during the war.

What accounts for this absence of hostility? One reason for it is that Jewish families were widely dispersed among the rest of the population, instead of being isolated either territorially or linguistically. The Bulgarian Jews did not live in ghettoes; some of them knew the Judeo–Spanish dialect, Ladino, but they all spoke Bulgarian. It was hard for their countrymen to see the Jews as the incarnation of evil, as the agents of some dark power; the face of the Jew that was familiar to most Bulgarians was altogether different: 'small grain merchants, pushcart vendors, retail tradesmen, labourers and maids, all of them working for a living and all of them going hungry' (p. 51). It was hard to foist on the Bulgarians the Nazi myth of the Jew as agent of worldwide exploitation.

There was also a second reason for this lack of hostility, having to do not with the Jews but with what might be called, for lack of a better term, the Bulgarian national character. German ambassador Beckerle refers to it on several occasions, in order to explain to his superiors the lack of anti-Semitic fervour in Bulgaria. 'I am firmly convinced,' he writes in a report of 7 June 1943, 'that the prime minister and the government desire – and are actively seeking – the final and irreversible solution to the Jewish question. Yet they are hindered in their efforts by the mentality of the Bulgarian people, who lack our ideological clarity. Having grown up among Armenians, Greeks, and Gypsies, the Bulgarian finds no defect in the Jews that might justify special measures against them' (*Oceljavaneto*, p. 259). The petition to the Assembly by the Bulgarian Writers' Union speaks of this same national trait, but from a different standpoint: our fathers still have fresh memories of the yoke of oppression, it says. How can we accept a law that would subjugate and reduce to conditions of slavery those who live among us (see p. 45)?

To use the terms 'yoke' and 'slavery' in Bulgarian is to invoke automatically the five centuries of Turkish domination (1396–1878) that could not but leave their marks on the collective memory and national character. During that period, the Bulgarians shared the fate of other minorities within the Ottoman empire – Greeks, Armenians, Wallachians, Serbs, Albanians, Jews, Gypsies, and others. All of these peoples, in order to survive, had to learn to bend, to temper their pride, to accept that they had to live with their companions in misfortune. Then came the Liberation – brought about, moreover, by the intervention of a third party, the Russians, in the Russo-Turkish War, not by the efforts of the Bulgarians themselves. In the new Bulgarian state, they found themselves once again alongside their companions in misfortune of yesterday, but now with a large Turkish minority – all those who could not or would not expatriate themselves to Turkey. Strong national pride is not a distinctive trait of the Bulgarians, as I said earlier, and there are times when one might wish it were. But in this instance, it seems to have been this very weakness that was responsible for their relative tolerance towards their own minorities, for their refusal to use them as scapegoats, for the absence of feelings of superiority over others, which is the first step in their subjugation or exclusion. Of course, having been a victim yesterday does not guarantee that individuals will not side with their oppressors today; indeed, one sometimes gets the impression that what those who have been injured want more than anything is compensation for their past suffering. But the absence of national pride – by which I mean in this case the conviction that one is a cut above people of other nationalities – combined with a capacity for self-criticism seem to have inoculated the Bulgarians against the temptation to make scapegoats of others.

Recent history seems to support this assessment. During the 1980s, the Communist government began to persecute the Turkish minority; one of the first measures taken against the Turkish Bulgarians was the Bulgarization of Turkish names. Far from being eagerly supported by the population, these measures instead provoked dissident movements, the first ever under the Communist regime. No other cause had had this effect, neither the suppression of public freedoms nor economic misery; it was not until a national minority was mistreated that a group of fellow Bulgarian citizens, who were not persecuted themselves, dared to say no.

Such was the soil in which political goodness, that rare and precious species, could take root. Let us now take a closer look at how these actions were carried out: what was it that made them succeed?

The answers to that question vary, depending on the level in the political hierarchy of the actors concerned. To start at one extreme, from the moment the king decided to stand firmly in the way of the deportation, he took the necessary and most appropriate measures. Rather than enter into direct confrontation with the German authorities, who could have engineered his overthrow, he placated them with vague promises, all the while placing obstacles in their path. The German ambassador to Sofia ended up advocating Boris's policies to his own government: a remarkable reversal. With his counsellors or subordinates, ministers or deputies, the king was always cautious; no one could claim to know exactly what his intentions were. With representatives of Jewish organizations, Boris was polite but distant; he gave them reassurances, without venturing, however, beyond general expressions of concern. He pulled all the strings but never took centre stage, leaving such easy gratifications to his ministers. He preferred the shadows to the light of day. Characteristically, after having changed the deportation order into an evacuation order, on 20 May 1943, he left Sofia to go hunting; in the days that followed, while the chancelleries were in a state of panic, the king remained inaccessible. There is no denying it: everything happened exactly as he intended.

Ordinary public figures did not have the same possibilities available to them; they had to content themselves with exerting pressure where they could, while trying to improve their chances of success. The proposed Law for the Defence of the Nation stirred the conscience of many. Professional and trade organizations – the Bulgarian Writers' Union, the Union of Lawyers, the Union of Doctors, the Union of

Artists' Societies, the Craftsmen Association – used measured terms in their letters of protest and did not neglect to stress their patriotism, but to little effect. Lawyers, deputies, and politicians correctly pointed out to the government that the new law contradicted not only the dictates of their consciences but the explicit provisions of the Constitution as well – again, to no avail. The metropolitans, who as stewards of the state religion were public figures, tried to show the conflict between the spirit of the law and that of Christianity; they were politely advised to mind their own business. Kazasov, in his open letter to Prime Minister Filov, showed great courage and trenchant wit; nevertheless, the law was passed and implemented. The good souls proved powerless, which does not mean that their actions were futile; but for the time being, the effect of those steps had yet to reveal itself.

The next crisis, centring on the deportation, was not unlike the first in this respect. Protests by public figures, by the high clergy, brought no results. There was only one exception, but it was major and for that reason it warrants discussion at length. I am referring to Peshev's action. What was exceptional about it? Not the fact that the man behind it obeyed the voice of his conscience rather than his government's order nor that he was ready to accept the risks that came with insubordination. What made his action unique was the simple fact that it succeeded.

Peshev's action consisted of a series of steps. The first was the visit on 9 March 1943 to Internal Affairs Minister Gabrovski. Here Peshev's stubbornness and firmness paid off, for initially Gabrovski claimed that no one had ordered any round-up of Jews (here, Gabrovski was essentially taking a leaf out of the king's book, telling each person what he wanted to hear). The deportation halted only because Peshev, Mikhalev, Ikonomov, and the other deputies refused to leave Gabrovski's office as long as he would not, in their presence, give the order to release all the Jews who had been arrested. Perhaps there seems something naive about this scene (could Gabrovski not cancel his order once his visitors had left?). Nevertheless, this direct, face-to-face interaction between the parties was essential. Peshev and his friends' insistence paid off.

Nothing had really been settled, however. Gabrovski had backed down, but he could change his mind; and behind him there was Filov, a man obsessed with power who hated to give ground. Peshev understood that now, after the first intervention, the crucial moment had come. 'I decided to act,' he writes in his memoirs, 'but how?' (p. 163). And so began the game of chess between two fearsome adversaries, Peshev and Filov.

Peshev analysed the situation lucidly. Quick action was necessary. He had helped forestall the deportation, but the government's decision – the reason for the deportation – remained in force. Public protests were useless, for they could always be brushed aside in the name of state interests. The government's position had to be reversed. Who could do it? Apart from the king, to whom Peshev did not have access, there was only one possibility: the National Assembly. The fact that Peshev was its vice-chairman and had friends there made the choice all the more compelling. Peshev's legalism, his attachment to the forms of democracy themselves, such as the Assembly, pushed him in this direction. What was also critical, Peshev saw, was that no one be able to discredit the action. Here Peshev made a second strategic choice: to decline the offer of help from certain members of the opposition party. The action against the government's decision must be led by members of the majority party, the party of government itself. It had to be absolutely clear that the deputies who were challenging the government's decision were acting in the name of the same goals and the same overall policy; that what they wanted was not to change the policy line but to show that it was being ill served by the government's recent decisions. Only in this way, Peshev reasoned, did their action stand a chance of succeeding.

Peshev immediately composed a protest letter to the prime minister and, at the next meeting of the Assembly, on 15 March, he began to circulate it among other members of the government majority. By 17 March he had already gathered forty-two signatures besides his own, and he decided that the time had come to show his hand. A week had passed since the meeting in Gabrovski's offices. Peshev took the floor and addressed the chairman of the National Assembly, who listened in silence and then left to see the prime minister.

It was only at this moment that Filov entered the picture; Peshev had a head start, which he would use to his advantage. Learning on 18 March of the existence of a letter of protest signed by forty-three deputies, Filov first tried stalling tactics: Peshev should not make his text public, but merely submit it at the next party caucus. Peshev received the message, but the contents aroused his suspicions. Why the further delay? Obviously, Filov feared publicity; his weakness therefore had to be exploited. By the next morning, 19 March 1943, Peshev had sent the protest letter through the prescribed legislative channels, thereby making it public, even though this haste may have cost him a few additional signatures.

Filov counter-attacked. He met with the king's adviser and laid out his own strategy. Rather than allow a debate on the Jewish question and risk an open airing of the divisions within the party, Filov would call for a vote of confidence on the government's policies as a whole; he felt sure he would win. 'I . . . made it clear that the vote of confidence had to be full and complete; in other words, that voting for the government on certain points and against it on others was out of the question' (p. 88). In the meantime, he tried to isolate Peshev by demanding that each signatory to the letter withdraw his signature. And finally, Filov suggested to a compliant deputy that he introduce a motion of censure against Peshev and call for his resignation from the vice-chairmanship. The king, who had himself adopted Peshev's position on the Jewish question, gave no indication of where he stood. 'The king agrees to the censure of Peshev by the majority,' writes Filov in his diary on 23 March, 'to prevent him from doing further damage' (p. 87).

Filov had thus managed to regain the initiative, and everything seemed to be going as planned. Then came the first snag. Not all of the forty-two deputies who had signed the petition recanted; thirty of them stood by their earlier decision. At the majority caucus, on 24 March, the vote of confidence was passed unanimously. Peshev had voted in favour as well, for he did not want to bring down the government, only to change its policies, which he had succeeded in doing. Nevertheless, when it came to the vote of censure against Peshev, the deputies were divided once more: sixty-six voted in favour, thirty-three against, and eleven abstained ('[his] friends, who had signed the letter, could not abandon him,' Filov explained, p. 89).

Peshev then played a new card. He refused to resign, even though that same night Filov had sent a mutual friend, who was also minister of justice, to see him, in order to convince him to take this step and spare himself further humiliation. Peshev refused categorically. To resign, voluntarily, would be to admit that what he did was wrong, and that was exactly what he did not believe. He thought he had been altogether right: 'It was my firm belief that I had done my duty' (p. 178). The next day, 25 March, Filov's men prevailed. The vote of censure was passed, and Peshev was removed from his post, without ever having been allowed to speak in his own defence. Filov won this little war of egos and overcame an adversary who, in any case, was not after total victory and lacked the means to achieve it.

But fundamentally, the victory was Peshev's. The deportation was interrupted and would not resume. Peshev had suffered some personal humiliation but knew that it was the price to pay, and well worth it. 'I was therefore entirely satisfied. My personal disappointments and my personal troubles in this story were insignificant by comparison' (p. 182).

Peshev had reason to feel proud. He and his allies, fighting for justice, had demonstrated that there was no such thing as a situation without a solution, that one did not have to resign oneself to one's fate. In the Europe of 1943, under Nazi control, he was probably the only statesman to have been able to stand up to infamy, to stop the persecution of the Jews. After him, no one can say, 'I didn't know, it wasn't my place, I couldn't have . . .'

What sets Peshev apart from other courageous and unselfish men was therefore not his conscience but his strategy. He did what had to be done under these particular circumstances in order to achieve his goal. The open protest, the rebellion within his own party that he managed to organize, was appropriate for Bulgaria in 1943. Under other circumstances, these same measures might have been futile, even suicidal. After 9 September 1944, open dissent carried much greater risks.

A case in point: during the war, Nikola Petkov was one of the leaders of the extra-parliamentary opposition, the Fatherland Front, an illegal anti-fascist organization, but he was not a Communist (he belonged to the Bulgarian National Agrarian Union). In this capacity, he signed a letter of protest addressed to the king concerning the evacuation of the Jews of Sofia to the countryside (p. 106); he was never harassed or attacked for having taken that action. After 9 September, he once again found himself among the opposition, now the democratic opposition to the Communist regime. That regime, however, was not as lenient as the previous, 'fascist' regime. Petkov was arrested, tried, and executed; his political group was dissolved and banned. He had done no more than Peshev had done, merely criticized certain government actions. But Bulgaria by this time had become a totalitarian state, which it clearly had not been under the king and Filov. Under a totalitarian regime, parliamentary action is no longer appropriate; dissent must find other courses of action.

Looking back and reflecting on the rescue of the Bulgarian Jews, one comes to realize that no one individual or single factor could have brought it about. Only concerted action made it possible. We would like, perhaps, to be able to name an individual and declare him hero of heroes, the champion of good against evil; in reality the responsibility was shared. The king, without the swell of public opinion against the deportation, and without the intervention of many around him, would not have decided to suspend it. Men of conscience and courage, men like Stainov and Kazasov, Stefan and Cyril, Ikonomov and Peshev, would have struggled in vain if the king had not decided to take their side; and they themselves would not have acted as they had if they had not felt that the Bulgarian citizens, with some few exceptions, stood behind them in their efforts. The people were opposed to the anti-Semitic measures, but a community is powerless without leaders, without those individuals within its midst who exercise public responsibility – in this case, the metropolitans, the deputies, the politicians who were ready to accept the risks that their actions entailed. All this was necessary for good to triumph, in a certain place and at a certain time; any break in the chain and their efforts might well have failed. It seems that, once introduced into public life, evil easily perpetuates itself, whereas good is always difficult, rare, and fragile. And yet possible.

DOCUMENTS

Exclusion

The documents in this part of the book date from 1940 to 1943. They have been divided into three sections, which correspond to three major moments in the history of the Bulgarian Jews during the Second World War: the exclusion of the Jews from Bulgarian society in 1940 by legislative means; the attempts to deport them, between February and March 1943; and, finally, their expulsion from Sofia and their house arrest, during the summer of 1943.

The texts in this first section concern reactions to the Law for the Defence of the Nation. This law was drafted in the ministry of internal affairs, for the most part by Alexander Belev, the future commissar for Jewish questions, who had been sent to Germany beforehand to study racial legislation. The law would first be presented to the public at a press conference on 8 October 1940 by the minister of internal affairs, Petâr Gabrovski; it would be introduced into the National Assembly in a first draft reading on 15, 19, and 20 November and in a second reading on 20 and 24 December 1940.

The law was greeted with numerous protests, a small sample of which are included here. From various sectors of Bulgarian society – professional organizations and trade associations, the Central Jewish Consistory and the Holy Synod, ordinary citizens and politicians alike – letters and protest statements were sent to the legislature and the administration. Nonetheless, the law was adopted and promulgated on 21 January 1941.

I

Statement by the Bulgarian Writers' Union to the Prime Minister and the Chairman of the National Assembly

22 October 1940

Dear Mr Prime Minister,

We, the undersigned Bulgarian writers, believe the time has come to present you with the following request:

On 8 October, statements by the minister of internal affairs were made public, and from these statements it appears that the government has decided to introduce in the National Assembly a proposal for a law, the Law for the Defence of the Nation. One can infer from these statements that the bill's objective is to deprive a Bulgarian national minority of its civil rights.

We are very surprised, and even embarrassed, by the fact that it has been deemed necessary to devise such a law when our nation is not being threatened or attacked by anyone.

In our opinion, such a law will be very harmful to our people.

Our legislature must not approve a law that will enslave one part of Bulgaria's citizens, and leave a black page in our modern history.

Many times in the past, our people have been subjected to persecution and humiliation. Our fathers still remember the shame of the foreign yoke. As our poet says, Bulgarian backs still bear 'the scars of the lash, the marks of suffering . . .'*

Should we then imitate these atrocities and follow a similar

---

*These lines are from a poem by Bulgaria's 'national poet', Ivan Vazov (1850–1921).

and dangerous road that will lead us to lose our place among the world's free and civilized peoples?

We are not defending this or that national minority; our aim is rather to uphold our country's reputation in the eyes of the civilized world. We would warn those on whom this depends that passing this bill will tarnish our country's reputation and soil its traditions of religious tolerance and humanity, won at so great a cost.

In the name of civilization and so as to preserve Bulgaria's good name, we ask you to stop the enactment of this law whose dire consequences will bring dishonour to our legislature and leave the saddest of memories.

Please accept the assurances of our respect.

T. G. Vlaikov	Mladen Isaev
Elin-Pelin	P. Gorianski
S. Chilingirov	Nikolai Liliev
K. Konstantinov	Miroslav Minev
Nikola Filipov	V. Rusaliev
Crisan Zankov-Derijan	Ilia Volen
Lyudmil Stoyanov	D. B. Mitov
G. Cheshmedjiev	Nikolla Djerov
Minko Genov	N. P. Ikonomov
Trifon Kunev	Ana Kamenova*
E. Bagryana	

---

*This list includes the names of most of the most prominent writers at the time, with the exception of the Communists. Grigor Cheshmedjiev is said to be the author of the text.

2

Statement by the Governing Board of the Bulgarian Lawyers' Union to the Chairman of the National Assembly

30 October 1940

Dear Mr Chairman,

The Bulgarian Lawyers' Union is extremely surprised to learn of the existence of a proposed Law for the Defence of the Nation. We have not seen the text of the draft bill itself, but statements made by the minister of internal affairs and taken up in the press on 9 October have made its general thrust sufficiently clear . . .

Nothing in the minister's statements indicates why our country now requires such a law. On the contrary, we learn from the minister's statements that he firmly believes the following: 'The Bulgarian state and the Bulgarian people have always striven to preserve the integrity of their national character and, most important, have been entirely successful in this regard. The Bulgarian state is wholly national and our nation has maintained its purity to a degree rarely attained in Europe.' Accordingly, if the minister himself – speaking, no doubt, for the cabinet – affirms that the Bulgarian state is wholly national and that our nation has maintained its purity, what national necessity could therefore justify the creation of a law that would restrict the rights of a category of Bulgarian citizens and morally degrade them? The Jews of Bulgaria have threatened neither our economy, nor our culture, nor the purity of the Bulgarian people. It would be totally erroneous to claim that the Jews wield any special influence over our cultural, political, or economic life. By the same token, it

47

would be entirely unjust to maintain that the Jews have done any less than our other fellow citizens to acquit themselves of their civic duties. That is why we can see no justifiable cause, from the standpoint of the interests of the state and the people, to impose such restrictive and humiliating measures on Bulgaria's Jewish minority. Not only are these measures unjustified, they also contradict the free and democratic spirit of the Bulgarian people, who, in all the long years of the Ottoman yoke and its miseries, misfortunes, and injustices, never considered the Jews their enemies or oppressors.

Furthermore, it should be mentioned in this regard that there are Bulgarian minorities today who are living under foreign domination, and their cruel fate has aroused the pain and indignation of our people.* Our concern, our struggles to defend these oppressed minorities will lose much of their judicial and moral foundations if we impose restrictions and arbitrary measures on a national minority here at home.

As lawyers, we owe it to ourselves to state that there are no professional reasons that might require the imposition of any restrictions whatsoever on our colleagues of Jewish extraction. As a group, they have always been upstanding members of our order and have always assumed their professional and moral duties as lawyers. Some, both in the past and still today, have served as members of the governing bodies of our organizations and institutions and have carried out the responsibilities entrusted to them with diligence and dignity. We resolutely oppose any and all attempts to restrict the rights of Jewish lawyers. Measures of this sort are absolutely harmful to the freedom of our profession.

Apart from all the above, what is and has always been most

*The allusion here is to parts of Thrace and Macedonia, which contained large populations of Bulgarian origin but which belonged at the time to Greece and Yugoslavia respectively.

important for us, as lawyers, are the legal aspects of this question. The proposed law constitutes a new attack on our basic legal principles. The Bulgarian Constitution expressly forbids the separation of Bulgarian citizens into inferior and superior categories. All Bulgarian citizens are equal before the law (Article 57). All Bulgarian citizens have political rights (to vote and hold elective office, to occupy civil and military positions, etc.), and all inhabitants of our kingdom have civil rights, that is, all of the rights specified in the civil code (Article 60). How are these basic legal principles to be reconciled with the above-mentioned restrictions planned for the Jewish minority in Bulgaria? It is clear that approval of the bill would be a violation of our Constitution, a violation that our ministers must not seek nor our representatives tolerate, for they have sworn to safeguard and defend the Constitution.

We therefore urgently ask you to abandon this bill, which is unnecessary, socially harmful, and contrary to our legal system and to all principles of justice.

For the governing board of the Union of Bulgarian Lawyers:

P. Boyadjiev, Chairman
N. Raichev, Secretary

3

Open Letter from Christo Punev* to the National Assembly Deputies

As deputies, you have a legal and moral duty: to defend the Constitution. This duty is unquestionable, as you know perfectly well, better than I. And so if I have resolved to write to you today, it is with this one goal in mind: that you and I, ordinary citizen though I am, might remember a few truths along with certain obligations that I, as governed, and you, as members of the governing body, have contracted voluntarily. Your actions cannot and must not violate the Constitution . . .

Let us reread . . . the Bulgarian Constitution and then ask ourselves the following question and answer it as honest Bulgarians: 'Why are we going to make outlaws of Bulgaria's Jews?' Before raising your hands to ratify a shameful and inhuman law, a law that goes against all civilized norms, you should have a look at the history of our people, their struggle for freedom . . .

One of the accusations made against the Jews by the more ill-informed members of the Bulgarian public is that they commit a certain crime called 'speculation'. Now it is an economic truism that 'to do business is to speculate'. And what is speculation? Speculation is buying a kilogram of tomatoes from the farmer and then selling them to one's brother in Sofia at five times the price. Speculators? Every nationality has its speculators, and then some. Jew, Bulgarian, French and

*Christo Punev was a journalist and a politician.

German, English and Italian, you'll find avid speculators among every people, for speculative capital knows no homeland! There is not a morsel of food left to buy in our markets, and they say it is speculation that is to blame. Well, then, just how many speculators are there among the Jews? The vast majority of Jews in Bulgaria are working-class people: small grain merchants, pushcart vendors, retail tradesmen, labourers and maids, all of them working for a living and all of them going hungry. Have you not walked by the children of Yuchbunar* on the streets of the capital? Little children and students, have you not seen them, famished, jaundiced, wasted and ragged, marching alongside Bulgarian children on Cyril and Methodius' Day? Have you not heard them, their voices hoarse, singing *Ô Dobroudja* and all the other songs of our nation's spirit at the top of their weak little lungs?†

Is it because of these children, these innocent souls who tomorrow will become an integral part of Bulgarian society, that today you are going to sow turmoil and fear in the house of their fathers with a law for 'the defence of the nation'? Poor Bulgaria! We are seven million people, yet we so fear the treachery of 45,000 Jews who hold no positions of responsibility at the national level that we need to pass exceptional laws to protect ourselves from them . . . And then what? Why should we need an exceptional law to protect the state, when there already exist legal sanctions against treason and felony, against speculation and every other possible type of crime? We have laws, hundreds and thousands of them, but where are the men who respect them in all conscientiousness?

Speculators? You, gentlemen, are our deputies, our country's primary and highest authority. Make laws then, seek out

---

*A working-class quarter of Sofia, home to many Jews of modest means.

†Hence they are good patriots: they are for the return of Dobrudja, which Bulgaria had been forced to cede to Romania under the 1913 Treaty of Bucharest, in the aftermath of the First Balkan War.

those who rob our people, and punish them; see that the laws are carried out ... You know better than we do, in Sofia, what King Rumour has been bruiting about, from Vidin to Burgas, from Petrich to Ruse: today he tells us that our country's economy is controlled by a hundred industrialists and by a hundred hunting dogs who circle the golden manna night and day! ...

But let us return to the subject at hand: you have been asked, in the days to come, to examine and approve a law against the Jews. What will you do? I can tell you now that if you believe in terror, if you think our country should be destabilized during the critical days ahead, at a time when what we need more than ever before is peace and harmony among all citizens living under our Bulgarian sky, then you will vote with the instigators and authors of this bill; but if you truly represent the people and their interests, you will strike this bill from the Assembly's calendar once and for all. Why? Because between now and then you will have heard what Bulgarians are saying; in the cities and in the countryside, they are all saying the same thing: 'If only Levski and Botev* were here today, they would make a whip out of the rope that hanged the Apostle; they would chase us down and flog us to make us understand their ideas and just what is this liberty in the name of which they died for Bulgaria ...'

Gentlemen. Decide now! Will you stand behind the Constitution and the Bulgarian people in defence of freedom, or will you march in step with the political mercenaries and bring shame on yourselves as you undermine our country's life and future along the way? There is no other alternative!

I am just an ordinary Bulgarian citizen, and so if I speak to you today, it is because I know in my heart that you too – sons

---

*Vasil Levski (1837–73) and Christo Botev (1848–76) were Bulgarian national heroes who died in the armed revolt against Turkish rule.

and grandsons of those who died for freedom on the gallows, on the hillsides and in the ravines of the Balkans, or on the executioner's block at Batak* – have not forgotten the oath they swore with their last breaths: Let us protect humanity and freedom!

All Bulgarian citizens capable of bearing arms swore and still swear to defend Bulgaria. And you, gentlemen, as deputies, you have sworn to do something else as well – to defend the Constitution!

Let each of us from the place he occupies accomplish his duty as citizen!

Christo K. Punev

The original document was also signed by the following individuals:[†]

Yanko Sakâzov, former minister
Dimo Kazasov, former minister
Ivan Runevski, attorney
Lyudmil Stoyanov, writer
Stoyan Kosturkov, former minister
Petko Stainov, professor
Konsantin Neftyanov, journalist[‡]

---

*A village where the Bulgarian insurrection against the Turks in 1876 was heavily repressed.

† This handwritten paragraph was added by Punev.

‡ All of these individuals belonged to the non-Communist opposition at the time.

53

4

Statement by the Holy Synod of the Bulgarian Orthodox Church to the Prime Minister

15 November 1940

Esteemed Mr Prime Minister,

... The Orthodox Church takes great interest in and has always been extremely satisfied with the efforts of our people and the Bulgarian government to protect our people and our country from the dangers that menace them from all sides. That is why our Church is particularly pleased to learn that the state intends, by means of the Law for the Defence of the Nation, to protect our people and all that is Bulgarian from such dangers. Nevertheless, [the Church] considers itself duty-bound, precisely for the good of the people, to alert those concerned to certain defects in the bill that has been presented, which may bring unfortunate consequences and therefore concern the Church in its capacity as a divine institution whose duty it is to look after its spiritual children and ensure that God's commandments are carried out so that justice and goodwill might triumph among men and nations.

This bill contains very grave provisions, but it also has gaps that open the door to many dangers that could jeopardize our nation.

To begin with, the bill makes no distinction between Israelite Jews and those Jews who, though of unbaptized parents, have personally adopted the Christian faith. It treats these Christians and the Israelite Jews in the same way. The Christians of Jewish origin, who have personally adopted the Christian religion five, ten, twenty years ago or more, are, by

54

their faith, by their religious and folk customs, by their language and by their culture, naturally linked with the Bulgarian people; they have severed their ties with the Jewish community and have assimilated into the Bulgarian people, yet this bill forcibly separates them from our people by placing them in the same category as the Israelite Jews. Clearly, such treatment is unacceptable. That is why our national Church is compelled to speak out in defence of its children who are bound both to it and, by their faith, to the Bulgarian people. If such a measure were in fact to be enacted, a portion of the Jewish population would be left with no other choice than to return to the Jewish religion; it would also make the future conversion of Jews to the Christian faith henceforth impossible.

The Church of Christ, which has received from its divine founder the eternal and imperious commandment to teach and to baptize in the name of the Father, the Son, and the Holy Spirit, to accept all men within its midst and point them the way to salvation, cannot agree to measures contrary to its divine mission of salvation and to the eternal commandment of its founder, Christ God. Such measures benefit no one, neither the Church nor our people, whose interests would be better served if they and men of other origins were united. Accordingly, the Bulgarian Orthodox Church, in accordance with the commandment of Christ the Lord, must oppose any measure that would stand in the way of those who wish to unite with it and with the Bulgarian people. Out of its sincere love and concern for its spiritual children, the Church will in the future take all legitimate measures to defend anyone who, whatever his origin, shall choose to adopt the Christian faith and join our people.

The Bulgarian Orthodox Church, whose duty it is to foster among our people the truth of salvation and the word of our Saviour in whose eyes all are children of one heavenly Father,

55

cannot neglect to call the attention of responsible individuals to the fact that, even in those of its clauses that target only Israelite Jews, the proposed law contains measures that cannot be considered just or useful for the defence of the nation. If there are dangers facing our nation, then the steps that are taken to counter them must target actions, not nationalities or religious groups; the proposed law, however, seems to have as its goal the special treatment of a Bulgarian national minority. All men and all peoples must defend their rights and protect themselves from danger, but this just aspiration must not serve as a pretext for injustice and violence towards others ...

For this reason and in view of the facts presented above, the Holy Synod, meeting in full assembly on 14 November, has decided to urge you, Mr Prime Minister, as well as the government and members of the National Assembly, to see to it that the proposed Law for the Defence of the Nation be modified and amended to include the following articles:

1. All Bulgarian citizens of Jewish origin who have adopted or will adopt the faith of the Bulgarian Orthodox Church shall enjoy the same rights as all Orthodox Bulgarians.
2. No actions shall be taken against the Jews as a national minority; however, specific measures shall be taken against any real danger, whatever its origin, that might threaten the spiritual, cultural, economic, social, and political life of the Bulgarian people.

The Bulgarian Orthodox Church, united with the Bulgarian people in a common destiny, discharging its spiritual duties according to the divine inspiration of the Gospel of Christ and the divine and eternal commandments, and having as its guiding principle not ephemeral and purely illusory material good but rather the lasting good of the Bulgarian people, would like to express its satisfaction with the state authorities who have protected the Bulgarian nation from a variety of dangers. [The Church] now deems it its further duty to stress these considerations and to urge you to modify and amend the proposed law as outlined above.

In so doing, not only will you be defending our nation, but you will also be safeguarding our reputation as a freedom-loving, just, and tolerant people.

We call on divine providence to bestow its blessings on you, and remain your ardent intercessors in our Lord Jesus Christ.

Grand Vicar and President of the Holy Synod,
Neofit of Vidin

5

Open Letter from Dimo Kazasov* to the Prime Minister

Dear Mr Prime Minister,

At this moment, you combine in your person five of the supreme functions of the political and cultural hierarchy. You are the prime minister of the Bulgarian government. You are head of the Bulgarian national educational system. You are president of the Bulgarian Academy of Sciences. You are a professor at Bulgaria's only university. You are president of the Bulgarian Pen Club.[†]

In virtue of this fact, everyone has the right to expect you not just to demonstrate political diligence and lucidity, but also to have respect for universal ethical norms, for the fundamental precepts of our national educational system, for scientific truth, for the important lessons that our nation's turbulent history has taught us, and for our literary patrimony. Everyone also has the right to expect you to show a heightened sensitivity to any attempt to condemn defenceless citizens to a moral death, incite the young generation to shameful violence, falsify historical facts, blacken the reputation of writers, political figures, scholars, and soldiers, and question the loyalty

*Dimo Kazasov, a portion of whose memoirs appear later in this volume, was a journalist, as well as a former and future member of the government. He was politically affiliated at the time to the non-Communist opposition.

†Prime Minister Bogdan Filov was in fact a scientist with an international reputation, who, following a brilliant academic career, became minister of education in 1938 and head of the government in 1940.

of any and all who are proud enough not to think like your friends.

It is with these expectations that I take the liberty to pose the following questions to you ...

With the permission of the censorship bureau that you control, a thousand copies of a tract were printed and distributed that charged a group of our most eminent writers, including Todor G. Vlaikov and Elin-Pelin, with corruption, for the simple reason that they had the courage to defend the Bulgarian Jews.*

Now there's a pretty picture: the dirt-mongers are protected by the censorship office while their victims – supposedly your fellows – remain in the custody of your indifferent silence!

Is it possible that the president of the Pen Club does not understand that writers who defend the Jews are at the same time defending the cultural originality of all Bulgarians, a people endowed with humanity, justice, and compassion for all those who suffer? Who knows better than the writers that Bulgaria, a poor, small country, can impose its will neither by force nor by wealth, and that our strength lies in our sense of justice and our wealth in our human qualities? When the Bulgarian people lose their sense of justice that they have nurtured over the course of centuries and that is so much a part of their national identity, they will lose their moral and spiritual uniqueness, their Slavic essence, their Bulgarian face. But that's not all. They will also lose a moral capital accumulated over many long years that has earned them a reputation as an industrious, tolerant, peaceful, just, and humane people. A defence of writers is a defence against any attempt to destroy what is most precious in the Bulgarian soul.

Surely the president of the Pen Club is aware that at

---

*Kazasov is alluding to the Statement by the Bulgarian Writers' Union to the prime minister and the chairman of the National Assembly.

congresses in Dubrovnik, Budapest, Barcelona, Prague, Buenos Aires, and so on, Bulgarian writers have sought the support of prominent international figures to ensure equitable treatment for the Bulgarian people, the Bulgarian language, and Bulgarian literature in countries where Bulgarians now live, just as we in Bulgaria have treated as our equals the national minorities living here. That support has been obtained. And so when Bulgarian writers stand up for the equal rights of Jews, they are standing by their honour and their signature to a moral contract with an organization for whom honour is neither an empty word nor a vain conceit.

Now I would like to ask Dr Filov, president of the Bulgarian Academy of Sciences and professor of the University of Sofia, how, with his anti-Semitic law, he intends to receive the world's congresses of scientists, writers, philosophers, painters, and composers, among whom the brilliant sons of the Jewish people occupy so eminent a place? The sciences in Bulgaria are still very young; do we really want to compromise them as well as our scientists because of the social hysteria that has upset the mental balance of some among us?

These brilliant sons of the Jewish people also play a leading role in the upper echelons of politics, economics, culture and science in countries everywhere. The war that is being waged here at home against the Jews will not pass unnoticed there: it will inevitably put us morally at odds with public opinion in these various countries, even as our national interests dictate that we maintain cultural as well as economic ties with them. Powerful countries, rich in both material and cultural resources as are the Germans and the Italians, can permit themselves the luxury of such discord, but small countries like ours must avoid it for their own good. We need all the friends, the compassion, and the help we can get. If anyone is to be accused of serving foreign interests, it is not those who have helped establish relations with others but rather those who would have those relations severed. What a strange and monstrous nationalism is this, to want to condemn one's people to complete isolation . . .

In a land like ours, so eager for the initiative and economic expansion that will allow us to uncover our hidden wealth and possibilities, you have unleashed a campaign against a national minority that is full of initiative, namely the Bulgarian Jews, who were born among us and live among us and die among us, leaving our country the fruits of their labour, and you relegate them to a moral status lower than that of the Gypsies . . .

You are waging war on Jewish capital, which, if one is to believe dubious statistics that are intended to present the Jews in the worst light possible, amounts to 486 million leva in stockholdings. It is the state that is sole master of this capital, because it belongs to Bulgarian citizens. But why do you overlook foreign capital, with its enormous, hidden influence, a capital totalling 1.8 billion leva, as against 2.9 billion of Bulgarian capital? Do you not see that the end result of this war against the Bulgarian Jews can only serve to raise foreign capital holdings in Bulgaria to an equal level with Bulgarian capital?

In the light of these and so many other facts, can you not see the strange hypocrisy that hides behind the struggle against foreign influence? Whom are you going to deceive as you try to conceal the fact that the struggle against the Jews and the Freemasons, who play no role at all in our social life, is in itself the result of foreign influences? There is only one way for you to keep the people confused on these and many other matters – with the gag and the whip. By means of these the president of the Bulgarian Academy of Sciences now proposes to watch over and safeguard the truth. But the truth will live again one day nevertheless, and in its light an astonished world will see that what the president of the Bulgarian Academy of Sciences was holding in his hand was not a torch but a whip.

6

Petko Stainov's* Speech in the National Assembly

19 November 1940

... And so, gentlemen, we come to the bill's second clause, which sanctions a number of important restrictions to which Bulgarian citizens of Jewish origin are to be subject. Two questions arise: first, are these restrictions constitutionally justified? And second, is the proposed law in our people's interest and in the spirit of their history and traditions? Let me dwell on these questions for a moment.

As to the first, I think that the proposed legislation violates our Constitution, particularly Article 57, which states that all Bulgarian citizens are equal before the law. Equality before the law is one of the fundamental preconditions of Bulgarian constitutional and public law ... Since our Constitution provides for equality among Bulgarian citizens, any measure that explicitly contravenes this provision is unconstitutional.

Gentlemen, there are other reasons why I will not raise my hand in favour of the bill in its present form. Under the pretext of defending the nation, the Law for the Defence of the Nation legally sanctions anti-Semitism, racism, religious inequality, and persecution. For the first time in our nation's history, certain citizens will be deprived of fundamental rights, on the basis of a Bulgarian *sui generis* racism. This, gentlemen,

*Petko Stainov, a member of the National Assembly, was a leader of the non-Communist opposition. After 1944, he became minister of foreign affairs.

is contrary to our history, to our National Awakening,* to our spirit, and to the dignity of Bulgarian people who are tolerant and honourable.

In singling out a group of people in order to assign them a particular status, and in restricting their basic rights, this bill, in Article 15, Paragraph A, relies, as I said, on a *sui generis* racism, one based on birth and blood. I do not subscribe to racial theories. Racial purity is a fairy tale. I do not believe in fairy tales and I am not about to draw conclusions of inequality among our citizens on the basis of an ill-founded theory of racism and racial purity, no matter how it is presented here. The term 'pure race' is a fiction. Who among us, knowing the history of this land, can say, 'I am racially pure'? . . .

And so we come to the second question. Can a law that would deprive Bulgarian citizens of their basic rights for ethnic or religious reasons, as this one does, serve the interests of the Bulgarian people? If it is in fact necessary to take certain measures, what kind of measures should they be? . . .

Are such measures necessary in Bulgaria? The Jews have never participated in Bulgaria's political or public life. There are no Jews in the Assembly – look around you. Nor are there any in the officer corps, in the theatre, in the press corps, in the telegraph agencies, insofar as we have any, nor in the diplomatic corps or the civil service. There were none yesterday and there are none today, and it has been this way for the last hundred years. But I do not have to tell you this, you know it already . . .

Since the Jews pose no threat, gentlemen, I do not see why we need to define new crimes and impose new restrictions. Article 17 of the Law for the Defence of the Nation forbids

---

*The National Awakening is the term that was given to the movement for national awareness in the nineteenth century, which preceded Bulgaria's liberation by the Russian Army and the creation of the modern Bulgarian state, in 1878.

Jewish participation in state affairs – but they have never participated in them in the first place.

7

Todor Polyakov's* Speech in the National Assembly

20 December 1940

Gentlemen,

In my opinion, the name that has been given to this bill is totally inappropriate, for the law will not do what its name suggests. What is more, I will refute the claim that the Jewish minority threatens the nation, and, consequently, that measures must be taken to defend it.

Forty-five thousand Jews live in Bulgaria today. One can state without hesitation that the Bulgarian people and the Jewish minority have lived in complete social and cultural harmony. Bulgaria's Jews were born here, it is here that they saw the sun for the first time, and the first language they heard was Bulgarian. They love our land, respect our laws, and are attached to our people and our state. They share our way of life: their houses, their cooking, and their behaviour are no different from ours. The youngest among them, products of our environment in every way, are totally assimilated. They speak and think in Bulgarian, have fashioned their style of thinking and their feelings after Botev, Vazov, Pencho Slaveikov, Yavorov, etc.[†] They sing Bulgarian popular songs and tell Bulgarian stories. Their private selves are modelled on ours – in the street, on our playing fields, at school, in the barracks, in workshops and factories, in the mountains and the

*Todor Polyakov was a Communist deputy.
[†] Here Polyakov cites the names of some of the greatest Bulgarian writers of the nineteenth and twentieth centuries.

fields; our sufferings are their sufferings, our joys their joys too.

To think that the Jews constitute a threat to our nation and our state is pure fantasy. They have never been involved in our country's political and public affairs. Other countries have persecuted Jews holding political and public office. This problem could never have arisen here, for in Bulgaria there are no Jews in the public administration, the army, the teaching corps, the state police apparatus, the judicial system, the theatre, the press, or the publishing industry. Consequently, the Jews have no possibility of exerting any influence whatsoever on our cultural and political life.

They are a weak minority who have never harmed us in any way whatsoever or threatened our identity or given anyone reason to think that they could threaten it in the future.

Nor can it be said that the Jews constitute a danger to us within the economic sector. The overwhelming majority of Bulgaria's Jews are working-class people, earning their livelihood in factories and workshops; some are artisans, retail merchants and employees; others are members of the liberal professions – lawyers, doctors, and dentists, who are as upstanding as they are hard-working. Jews involved in the commercial sector tend to own medium-sized businesses ...

For this reason, it would be unwise, unjustified, and cruel to single them out and restrict their right to earn a living.

Some people would like to portray the Jews as an amoral and criminal social element. That is a total fabrication. No nation has a monopoly on criminal behaviour. Good qualities and bad qualities are characteristics of individuals, not of nations. What social or political group does not include criminals, both petty crooks and major felons? What flock does not have its black sheep? I will even go so far as to say there is less criminality among the Jewish minority than among any other Bulgarian national group. If our official statistics are to be trusted, there were 12,923 violent crimes (murders and aggravated assaults) committed between 1920 and 1935; thus, if the rate of criminality among the Jews was 0.85 per cent, there should have been 110 crimes committed by Jews; in fact there were only 14. The same holds true for burglaries and the rest. The rate of illegal currency trading among the Jews may have been higher, but that is due to their relatively greater participation in this economic sector, given that they do not take part in the others . . .

We used to be able to tell ourselves that all this was a thing of the past, but if we enact a law such as this one, we will have to undo centuries of social progress and return to the infamous Middle Ages when Jews wore yellow badges on their clothing, and were persecuted and robbed to line the pockets of kings and their vassals. Men have risen above that in modern times. As Gorky says, 'Man: how proud that sounds.' We no longer consider it acceptable to inflict cruelty on animals, yet now we are about to reduce thousands of innocent and law-abiding people to the status of half-men, of second-class citizens, a status far lower than that of any other minority, be it Turkish, Greek, Armenian, or Gypsy. Right now, in the Bulgarian National Assembly, whose authority derives solely from the Constitution, a horrifying and anti-constitutional law is being drafted, a shameful page of our history is being written.

And why? Are the people demanding these measures? No. Bulgarians are tolerant, hospitable, good; intolerance towards Jews is alien to them. Our working class harbours no such feelings.

The Bulgarian intelligentsia is to be commended: lawyers and doctors, writers, and even some retired military officers and members of the reserve, and disabled servicemen as well, have taken public positions against this law. Our peasants do not think that Jews are trampling their fields, our lawyers do not complain of any unfair and disloyal competition . . .

But then why is this law being proposed? That question troubles many of us, and so we have to ask ourselves whether it just might be that it is being imposed on us by foreigners and by foreign interests. For the sake of my country's honour, I will not believe that this is the case. But one thing is certain: this bill is the result of foreign propaganda ...

If not for foreign propaganda, it would never have occurred to anyone to take such draconian and retrograde measures. We find it everywhere – on the radio, in books and newspapers; travellers are bringing it back home with them from abroad. And now it has reached sweeping proportions.

Germany and Italy are not the only countries that are dealing with the Jewish question; every country is doing so. So, consider, gentlemen, the way the Soviet Union is dealing with it. In the Soviet Union, the national question is one of vast dimensions. It is not only the Russians, the Ukrainians, and the Byelorussians who live and work there, but also the Finns and the Lithuanians, the Letts and the Estonians, the Armenians, the Chuvashians, the Mordvinians, the Ossetians, the Buryats, the Mongols, the Georgians, the Tatars, the Bashkirs, and dozens of other populations of every size. They all have their own languages, their national characters, their myths, their songs, their legends, their styles and so on. In the Soviet Union, the government believes that all these peoples can fulfil their national potential, and it does everything possible to nurture that potential. And public opinion is with the government on this matter.

Several million Jews live in the Soviet Union. They are everywhere – in Birobidjan, Moscow, Kiev, Odessa, Kishinev, and every other corner of that huge country. In the Soviet Union, Jews are equal to all other citizens before the law, both officially and in practice. Jewish national literature is encouraged: recently, the Soviet Union celebrated the birthday of Sholem Aleichem; it also fosters the efforts of Jewish writers, those who write in the Jewish dialect, like Markish and Kvitko, as well as those who write in Russian, like Marshak, Pasternak, Svetlov, and Ilya Ehrenburg, every one of them 100 per cent Jewish and more attached to Soviet society than anyone . . .

If you want to see how others are dealing with the Jewish question, do not just look at Germany; look how it is being resolved elsewhere.

Do not allow this proposed law to stain the reputation of the Bulgarian people, for if you do, the shame will be yours tomorrow.

As I said before, I think we should change the name of the bill, for in reality, it is not a law for the nation's defence but rather a proposal for its infamy.

Deportation

The texts I have compiled in this second section deal with the crucial episode of 1943: the attempt to deport 20,000 Bulgarian Jews. This operation, undertaken at the insistence of Eichmann's envoy, Theodor Dannecker, was directed by the Commissariat for Jewish Questions, headed by Alexander Belev, and was supported by the cabinet. Hostile reactions to the operation were not confined to the Assembly chambers; they also took place in the street. Examples of the former, which appear here, include the letter of protest signed by Peshev and co-signed by forty-two other deputies from the government majority, which cost Peshev his vice-chairmanship and earned him a vote of censure; that document is followed by a communication from Petko Stainov, of the liberal opposition, which is concerned in particular with the Jews deported from the newly acquired territories of Thrace and Macedonia.

These two texts are preceded by two documents from the underground press. The newspaper *Otechesvtven Front* (the *Fatherland Front*) was an organ of the group of that same name. The Fatherland Front was led by Communists but included other anti-fascist forces. A commentary on a Radio Moscow broadcast on the persecution of the Jews is the second document. This tract was distributed by the Sofia District Committee of the Workers' (i.e., Communist) Party.

The excerpts from the diary of Bogdan Filov (1883–1945)

are an exception in our choice of documents, as they reflect thoughts and opinions of those party to the persecution, rather than the efforts of those who tried to save the Jews. Filov's diary entries are valuable, however, for they shed light on the events of March 1943. Filov had had a brilliant scholarly and academic career, as a specialist in ancient history and archaeology. It was only in 1938 that he first joined the government, as education minister. New to politics though he was, he used his intellectual qualities and political resolve to his advantage. In a subsequent cabinet reshuffling, he was named prime minister, a post he retained until September 1943, when, after Boris's death, he became one of three regents. In the aftermath of the Communist takeover in September 1944, Filov was arrested and sentenced to death. In 1945, he was executed by firing squad.

In matters concerning the Jews, he took a hard line. In his exchange with the Swiss chargé d'affaires Charles Rédard, in which the latter tried to negotiate the departure of Jewish children to Palestine, one can also see that in Bulgarian ruling circles there was a clear awareness, if not an open admission, of the fate of the Jews who were deported to Poland.

The final document in this section is the dispatch by Charles Rédard to the Swiss government in Berne.

I

Article from the *Fatherland Front*

31 December 1942

After its complete coverage of the news, Radio Moscow addressed a worldwide appeal on behalf of the Jews and protested at the barbaric and inhuman extermination of Europe's peaceful Jewish population by the Germano-Italian fascist gangs.

Sensing that their end is near, Hitler and his satellites and satraps have lost all restraint. Hitler recently declared that he will exterminate and liquidate all of Europe's Jews. He has already begun to execute this plan. Never in history have greater cruelties and more barbaric acts been perpetrated against a European national minority than those being committed by German fascism against the Jews. The facts are terrifying. In Poland, out of 4 million Jews, only 40,000 are still alive: 3,960,000 have been exterminated ... The Jews of Serbia, Greece, France, Belgium, Holland, Norway, Poland, Bohemia, and other countries have been crowded into the Polish ghetto ... The extermination of Jews has begun in France, in Norway, in Holland. Thousands of brave French and Norwegians of all ages have died in rallies and demonstrations against it. Sweden's protest against these acts of unprecedented barbarity has been resolute. In Moscow, people from all over the world – English, Americans, Norwegians, Serbs, Greeks, Czechs, Poles, Dutch, Estonians, Letts, Russians, and others – have joined together and formed a committee for the defence of the Jews. In Hungary, all Jews who have in worked in the Kommandos and in the concentration camps have been assembled and exterminated. Hundreds of thousands of Jews have been massacred by the rabid fascist gangs in 'experiments' or in their crematory ovens where they have tried out their toxic gases. Jews have been killed by electrocution as well. Still others have been poisoned . . .

The Allies have vowed to avenge the innocent Jews from currently occupied Soviet territories in Europe who are still being massacred by the barbaric and savage Germano-Italian fascist gangs.

On Hitler's orders, the Bulgarian government has begun to pursue an obscurantist fascist policy against Bulgaria's Jews. It is now forbidden for them to work or reside in certain neighbourhoods; they are being subjected to humiliations of all sorts and are being forced to spend six months a year in work camps, where they face the ever-present risk of being exterminated, or, what amounts to the same thing, of being sent to a Polish ghetto.

Jews! Come join the brave ranks of the Fatherland Front! Take your place in the vanguard of the Bulgarian people's fight against odious fascism! Only the Fatherland Front can eradicate fascist obscurantism and racial hatred and rescue you from the horrors of fascism.

2

A Leaflet of the Sofia District Committee of the Workers' Party

[1942]

Dear compatriots,

The Hitlerite clique, led by King Boris, are conspiring against the Bulgarian people and preparing unspeakable atrocities. Disaster is imminent . . .

Anti-Semitism is out in full force. No human law, no human value could sanction the schemes it has inspired. The Law for the Defence of the Nation, the work camps, the confiscation of property, the yellow star, the denial of the Jews' right to work and to exist, these are but one link in the chain of savagery and inhumanity perpetrated by the Bulgarian fascists. Never before, since Bulgaria became a nation, has our Jewish population been subjected to such barbarity and evil as today.

Bulgaria's fascists want us to believe that by persecuting the Jews, by confiscating their property and taking away their right to work, they are battling speculation and fighting for the good of the Bulgarian people. But we can see with our own eyes that the confiscation of Jewish property serves only one purpose – to enrich the fascist bigwigs and feed the Nazi war machine. Speculation and the black market are thriving as never before. Having received half a million marks from Hitler, General Jekov has now set himself up in Landau's villa in Knyajevo* . . .

*General Nikola Jekov (1864–1945) was at that time honorary president of the Union of Legionnaires, an extreme-right organization. Knyajevo is a residential suburb of Sofia.

Dear compatriots, the fate of Bulgaria's 40,000 Jews and that of our people are intertwined. Do you seriously believe that the Nazis have not plundered our peasants and producers? Haven't our treaties given Hitler the equivalent of 15 billion leva in goods, a credit that we will never see again? Aren't our peasants, workers, artisans, and civil servants dying of hunger along with their families? Can you not see that the Nazi criminals have crushed our people's freedom?

It is not the Jews but Hitler and his gang who have pushed us into war against the peace-loving peoples of England and America.*

It is not the Jews but King Boris and his clique who have put Bulgaria's independence up for sale.

It is not the Jews but Germanized traitors like King Boris[†] who are getting us ready for a war against the Russian people, our brother Slavs to whom we owe our freedom.[‡]

It is not the Jews but King Boris and his stooges who are bent on throwing us into a war against Turkey, to force it to align itself with the new order, this order that the Hitlerite bandits have established.

It is not the Jews but today's Nazis as well as King Boris's father who have dragged Bulgaria into two national catastrophes and are now preparing a third and even greater one.**

Bulgarians, Jews: join in the common struggle against the despicable Hitlerite Bulgarian government under which we are all suffering equally! Create defence and resistance committees to fight the violence and atrocities perpetrated

---

*Since December 1941, Bulgaria was formally at war against Britain and the United States, but for the moment the declaration of war was of no practical consequence.

†Boris's father, Ferdinand, Bulgaria's preceding king, was a Saxe-Coburg-Gotha, and thus of German origin.

‡Here the author of the pamphlet alludes to the Russo-Turkish War of 1877–8, which led to the creation of the modern state of Bulgaria.

**See p. 5.

against the Jews. Do not move into the houses and apartments that were taken from the Jews by force! Do not let the Jews be forcibly expelled to the Gypsy quarter and surrounded by barbed wire. Show your solidarity with the Jews and your hatred for the Hitlerites!

Fight for the programme of the Fatherland Front, for freedom, democracy, and equal rights for all of Bulgaria's peoples, including the Jews!

Death to fascism! Liberty for all peoples!*

---

*This is the ritual formula with which all Communist documents from the period closed.

3

Protest Letter by the Vice-Chairman of the 25th Session of the National Assembly, Dimitâr Peshev, and Forty-two Other Deputies

17 March 1943

Esteemed Mr Prime Minister,

The great sense of historical responsibility we share with the government in these critical times, our steadfast loyalty to the regime and to its policy, as well as our desire to do all we can to ensure its success, give us the courage to address you, hoping that you will recognize the sincerity and goodwill of our action.

Recent actions taken by the authorities make clear their intentions to take new measures against persons of Jewish origin. What is the precise nature of these steps? On what basis are they being taken, and what is their motivation and scope? Explanations from responsible circles are missing. In a conversation with certain deputies, the minister of internal affairs confirmed that no exceptional measures against the Jews from the old territory were being contemplated. After that conversation such measures were actually cancelled.

Taking all this into consideration and in view of new rumours, we have taken it upon ourselves to appeal to you directly, for if such measures are carried out, it will have to be on the orders of the Council of Ministers. Our sole request is that before any measures whatsoever are undertaken, the real interests of the state and nation, and the good name and moral standing of the Bulgarian people, be taken into account.

We could never oppose measures taken by the government

to ensure the country's security, for we recognize that anyone who at this decisive moment in our history would obstruct the sovereign will of the government and the people, directly or indirectly, must be deprived of the power to do so. Indeed, the government is duty-bound to eliminate any and all obstacles to the success of its policy to which we have consciously lent our full support and on which we have proudly staked our reputation.

The right of the state to remove all obstacles that might stand in the way of its policy cannot be contested, so long as its actions do not go beyond what is truly necessary or fall into excesses that qualify as needless cruelty. Yet how else is one to describe measures taken against women, children, and the aged, people who are guilty of no crime whatsoever?

It is impossible for us to accept that plans have been made to deport these people, even though ill-minded rumours attribute this intention to the Bulgarian government. Such measures are unacceptable, not only because these people – who are still Bulgarian citizens – cannot be expelled from their own country, but also because this course of action would be disastrous, with grave consequences for our country. Our nation's reputation would be stained for ever, its moral and political standing for ever compromised, and thus the arguments that Bulgaria might one day need to rely upon in its dealings with foreign powers would lose all their force.*

Small nations cannot dispense with such arguments, which, whatever the future may hold in store, will always remain a powerful weapon, perhaps the most important weapon they have. This concern is particularly relevent for us today, for as our esteemed prime minister surely recalls, recent infringements of human rights and moral laws by certain Bulgarians

*This is an obvious allusion to the negotiations with the Allies that Bulgaria would enter into in the case of a German defeat.

and other individuals who have often acted irresponsibly have had serious political and moral repercussions for our country.

What Bulgarian government would be williing to accept this responsibility?

The small number of Jews in Bulgaria, the strength of our own state, with so many legal means at its disposal, make the elimination of any dangerous elements easy, whatever their origin. For this reason, we are deeply convinced that the use of exceptional and cruel measures, measures that may expose the government and the entire nation to accusations of mass murder, are unwarranted and excessive. The consequences of this policy would be particularly grave for the government, but they would weigh upon the Bulgarian people as well. These consequences can be easily foreseen, and for this reason the policy is inadmissable. We cannot share any responsibility for it whatsoever.

Good government requires basic legal principles, just as life requires air to breathe.

The honour of Bulgaria is not just a matter of sentiment, it is also and above all a matter of policy. It is of immense political capital and no one has the right jeopardize it without good reasons approved by the whole nation.

We beg you, Mr Prime Minister, to accept our deep esteem.

[Signed by forty-two deputies]

4

Petko Stainov's Interrogatory, Sent to the Prime Minister and Minister of Foreign Affairs, Bogdan Filov

22 March 1943

Esteemed Mr Prime Minister,

According to news arriving from Sofia, it appears that the authorities have forcibly assembled all Jews – women, men, children, and old people – from the territories acquired in 1941. Without allowing them to put their personal affairs in order and prepare their baggage, or even take enough blankets and clothing, the police have put these people on train wagons bound for Gorna Djumaya and Dupnitsa, where they were crammed into tobacco warehouses and left for several days in the cold and under the harshest conditions.

While this was happening, Jews from Plovdiv, Kyustendil, Pazardjik, and other towns were expelled from their homes under the same conditions and forcibly assembled in makeshift centres; yet subsequently they were freed, without ever having been told why they had been arrested or whether their freedom was provisional or definitive.

We have now learned that thousands of Jews – women, men, children, and old people – have been sent to Lom in sealed freight wagons. They have not been allowed to disembark at station stops nor exchange any communications with relatives or friends. Since yesterday, they have been waiting in these wagons at the port of Lom, exposed to the cold, thrown together like animals, with no idea where they are being taken.

Early this morning, these Jews have been put on board

barges on the Danube and are being sent to an unknown destination.

In view of these events, I am hereby asking for a debate in the National Assembly to discuss the forcible delivery to a foreign power of persons of Jewish origin residing in Bulgaria. I am also requesting that you please answer the following questions:

1. Is it true that the authorities have forcibly assembled all Jews from the new territories, except those who were previously naturalized as citizens of foreign countries?

   If so, do you not agree that, in the light of the general war being waged against the Jews and preached in official circles, this exception is tantamount to a capitulation to the foreign Jews?

2. If the government moreover considers these Jews not to be Bulgarian nationals and refuses to grant them Bulgarian citizenship (although all Turks, Albanians, Greeks, Armenians, and other minorities can opt for this until 31 April 1943), why did the government not allow them sufficient time to arrange their personal affairs and leave the territories for the country whose citizenship they would have chosen, instead of forcibly removing them from their houses without any warning?

3. Would you please tell me whether these Jews who have been placed aboard barges in the port of Lom are Bulgarian citizens or foreign nationals? If they are Bulgarian citizens, then even though they are of Jewish origin, the Bulgarian government has no right to extradite them or deliver them to a foreign power. If, on the other hand, they are foreign nationals and have been forced to leave Bulgarian territory, it must be that some foreign government has so demanded; in that case, anyone being expelled must be allowed to depart for the country of which he is a citizen or for another country of his choosing. In the case at hand, the Jews in question are the Jews of Thrace; if indeed they have not become Bulgarian citizens, they should be sent

directly to Greece, where they remain citizens, instead of being put onto barges on the Danube.

4. If the Jews are indeed being transferred from our territory and delivered to a foreign power and if this action falls within the purview of a convention between Bulgaria and that power, is it not the case that such a convention also needs to be approved by the National Assembly? Or is depriving living human beings – women, men, children, and old people – of their freedom or delivering them by force to a foreign power so trivial a matter that it need not be ratified by the people's representatives?

5. Given that it is going to be decided that the territories of Thrace and Macedonia are an integral part of the Bulgarian state and that, on more than one occasion, the National Assembly has considered them to be thus, there is reason to wonder whether certain paragraphs of the decree concerning citizenship in the new territories are in conformance with international law: the intent of these paragraphs seems to be to take away the right to choose either Bulgarian citizenship or foreign citizenship from individuals living in these territories and residing there permanently as local citizens, who in this case, for example, happen to be persons of Jewish origin living in these territories. Would you please tell me of what country these people are citizens, according to this decree?

I respectfully request that, pursuant to Article 107 of the Constitution and Article 63 of the Code, you indicate to the National Assembly on what day you propose to place this interpretation on the agenda and have it examined by the deputies.

Please accept the expression of my esteem.

P. Stainov

5

Bogdan Filov's Diary

17 February 1943. Tuesday. Audience with the king ...
Regarding Lukov's assassination,* I explained to the king that
it is not enough to say it was committed by 'foreign hands', or
by 'enemies of Bulgaria'. These formulas are very vague and
unconvincing and people will suspect the government. People
want concrete facts. We must focus on the real assassins, the
Communists undoubtedly, because the inquest has established
that Lukov was killed by the same person and the same
revolver that killed the carpenter a few days ago.† We must
take advantage of these assassinations to reinvigorate the
struggle against Communism and Jewry; of course, we mustn't
go to extremes and maybe we cannot do any better than we are
doing now, but the government must at least give the
impression that it will not tolerate such provocations and is
committed to taking the strongest measures possible. The
important thing now is the political effect.

I used this occasion to remind the king that two days ago
Beckerle informed me that sending 4000 Jewish children and
500 Jewish adults to Palestine, as was being discussed with the
English government (through the intermediary of the Swiss
legation), is not something that the British government will

---

*General Christo Lukov, president of the Union of Legionnaires, was
assassinated by the Resistance on 13 February 1943.
†An agent provocateur who was also killed by the Resistance.

look favourably on; such an action will be used as pro-English propaganda and will make the Arabs unhappy, something the Germans want to avoid. I had to agree with him. I also reminded the king of what Paul Schmidt had said to Zagorov in Berlin* about the Germans' attitude toward our government: the Germans, it seems, do not want to meddle in our affairs and are ready to support any government capable of dealing both with the Communists and the Jews, for whom there can be no place in the new Europe, and with the street, in other words, with other political movements, whether leftist or nationalist. The king agreed with me, although he did not seem particularly convinced by my argument . . .

After [Mikhov],† I called Gabrovski in too; together we analysed the situation thoroughly and made the following decisions:

1. Begin a newspaper campaign against the Communists and the Jews, while tightening repressive measures against them.
2. Post a large reward for the discovery of Lukov's killers . . .

11 March. Thursday. Today, I received a visit from Rédard, who wanted to speak to me about sending Jewish children to Palestine. He gave me a telegram to read which called for the creation of a committee of three Jews who would specify which children to send. I told him that this was unacceptable and that we reserved the right to choose the children. But before that, the technical problems raised by this action would need to be resolved. He proposed that we begin with a group of 100 children that the minister of internal affairs had agreed on, which would require two wagons. The discussion then

*Paul Schmidt was the press secretary for the German foreign ministry. Slavcho Zagorov was the Bulgarian ambassador to Berlin.

†Nikola Mikhov (1891–1945), minister of war and future regent, was later tried by the People's Tribunal and executed.

turned to the Jews we are deporting from the new territories. He offered to send a telegram to get them all admitted into Palestine. I replied that it was too late – they were leaving in a few days. He asked where they were going and I replied, 'To Poland,' to which he replied, 'That means to their death.' I explained that his conclusion was exaggerated; they would be used as workers, the same as the Bulgarians we were sending to Germany. He said it was not the same, that we were behaving inhumanely toward the Jews. I replied in a firm tone that this was no time to talk of humanity, while the peaceful populations of large cities were being massacred. He immediately agreed with me, mentioning the recent British air raids over Rennes, in Brittany, even though the city had no war industries and or strategic importance. We both agreed that the war was growing crueller by the day. I emphasized the harmful influence of the Jews here at home and I told him it was our right to defend ourselves, especially since there was still the possibility of Bulgaria's becoming a theatre of military operations. We have always been an extremely tolerant people, but now we are forced to take measures that we would certainly not adopt in normal times.*

15 March. Monday. Audience from 4:30 to 6:30 p.m. We talked mostly about the Jewish question and the king's attitude is still firm. We also discussed the debates in the cabinet, where I have often had to impose various points of view, something the king approved of totally, even if this results in resignations.

19 March. Friday. This morning I received a petition on the Jewish question from D. Peshev, signed by forty-three deputies, even though yesterday Peshev, at my request, had

---

*For Rédard's account of this meeting, see p. 92.

promised Kalfov* that he would not send it to me before speaking with me. This is an important development and there are going to be consequences. Now I truly realize the extent of Jewish influence and how harmful these people really are. Toward noon, several deputies, led by S. Vasilev,† came to me to complain about this petition. I told them that the matter was of great importance and that a majority caucus would be held to determine the various consequences.

20 March. Saturday. After my meeting with Sevov,‡ we examined Peshev's letter in the cabinet. Mainly at my insistence, we decided to use it as a test case for the majority, calling for a vote of confidence, insisting on Peshev's removal as vice-chairman, and ejecting from the majority those who refuse to withdraw their signatures. The time is right because the legislative session is nearing its end, and, moreover, the Jewish question would make a good subject for a campaign platform, if it should come down to holding new elections. Of course, the government could also fall, but I stated bluntly that I would prefer a smaller but safer majority to one that might compromise the government at any time. P. Kyoseivanov came to see me today to withdraw his name in writing. Yesterday evening, Spas Marinov** came to see me and said he was withdrawing his as well, but I insisted that he do it in writing . . .

23 March. Tuesday. This morning, I went to see the king . . . The king agrees to the censure of Peshev by the majority, to prevent him from doing further damage.

*Christo Kalfov was chairman of the National Assembly, of which Peshev was vice-chairman.

†Slaveiko Vasilev, a deputy from the majority.

‡Yordan Sevov, an architect, was a personal adviser to the king.

**Petâr Kyoseivanov was a majority deputy and ambassador to Berne; Spas Marinov was another deputy.

24 March. Wednesday. Majority caucus to discuss Peshev's letter on the Jewish question. After difficult and protracted debates, in the course of which I reproached Peshev for his improper attitude, I called for a vote of confidence and for Peshev's censure. All 114 deputies present voted their full support of the government on all points, including the measures against the Jews. It was also emphasized that Peshev's letter, signed by forty-three persons, would be considered withdrawn. On the question of Peshev's censure, the majority was divided: sixty-six voted for, thirty-three against, and eleven abstained. Four deputies left the meeting before the ballot: Sotir Yanev, Serafim Georgiev, Dr Durov, and S. Chalburov. They wanted to have a 'clear conscience'. P. Kyoseivanov, who had withdrawn his signature from Peshev's letter in writing, did not attend. After the vote, Peshev, though urged to resign, refused to do so, declaring pathetically that he was the one who had written the letter, that he had done so on his own initiative, and that he took full responsibility for it. After the vote, Peshev started to argue with me. He intimated that I would live to regret this action. I told him that everyone had to take responsibility for his own actions and I finished with the words – 'Tu l'as voulu, Dandin,'* – implying that he had been asking for it for a long time. Indeed, I had called the meeting in order to expose Peshev, and the outcome was a complete success. Everyone understood that Peshev wanted to hurt the government and, if not bring it down, then at least compromise it. This did not keep him from voting yes in the vote of confidence. I had made it clear that the vote of confidence had to be full and complete; in other words, that voting for the government on certain points and against it on others was out of the question. Under these conditions, Peshev's vote contradicted his earlier vote, because I had

*From Molière's *Georges Dandin*: 'You asked for it, Dandin.'

stated that the government asked for a vote of confidence on Peshev's replacement as well. Nevertheless, I did not want to make this an issue, because the second vote related to a person; and Peshev's friends, who had signed the letter, could not abandon him. Similarly, I did not want to confuse these two problems, because what I wanted was consensus on our policies.

26 March. Friday. At today's session in the chamber, the first order of business was Dr Popov's motion to censure Peshev. The motion was accepted without debate, which caused an uproar among the opposition and was protested against by Peshev's friends. Soon afterwards, however, when the debate had shifted to a decision about the new territories, the speakers brought up Peshev's censure, its motives, and its relation to the Jewish question. Peshev made a big mistake by refusing to step down because now everyone will think he was censured because he defended the Jews. When T. Kojukharov* spoke, he attacked me as well. He said that that Petko Stainov had referred to me as a benign dictator, but in fact, it seemed to him that I was a true dictator with an iron hand but that I only used it in the National Assembly. He said he would like to see an iron hand like this used everywhere, for example, in the failure of the potato affair, in which case he would kiss that iron hand on both sides . . .

5 April. Monday. Audience with the king at five o'clock. He is unhappy with his visit to Hitler. He did not get a favourable impression . . . .. He discussed the Jewish question with Ribbentrop at length, trying to explain to him that Bulgaria's Jews are

---

*Todor Kojukharov was a member of the rightist opposition in the Assembly. He, along with fellow rightist opposition deputy Alexander Tsankov, signed Peshev's letter, but unlike Tsankov, who would manage to emigrate, Kojukharov would be executed in 1945.

Spanish [i.e., Sephardim] and that they in no way play the role they do in other countries. But it seems that Ribbentrop did not accept these objections and replied that a Jew is always a Jew. Spain's attitude was also the cause of some displeasure. Apparently, Hitler intends to erect a third barrier against a Balkan front: the islands, Greece, and the Bulgarian line ...

13 April. Tuesday. At five in the afternoon, Gabrovski and I went to the king's ... We discussed the Jewish question. The king is of the opinion that we ought to put all able-bodied Jews in work camps in order to avoid sending the Jews from old Bulgaria to Poland. The king noted that there seemed to be some disagreement between Gabrovski and me, since Gabrovski said he wants the Consistory to include baptized Jews, something I fiercely oppose, lest we upset the Holy Synod ...

15 April. Thursday. I was at the Vrana residence at a quarter to ten, where the king and I waited for the metropolitans – Neofit, Stefan, Sofroni and Paisi – to arrive ... Our conference with the metropolitans began at ten o'clock exactly. The king gave a good and detailed account of the Jewish question, stressing the fact that it was not a specifically Bulgarian problem but a European one.* Neofit and Stefan then took the floor, and mainly defended the converted Jews. I pointed out that in this matter, there was no difference of opinion between the government and the Synod, and I underscored the fact that the matter would already have been resolved were it not for Stefan's circular, in which he wrote that 'his soul rejoices'. He admitted that it was a mistake on his part not to have asked me how to announce the government's intentions to the converts. I pointed out that when dealing with these problems, one cannot put things down in writing,

*See the transcript p. 102.

and I noted that the general mood in the chamber was unfavourable towards the Jews and that the proposals made on their behalf to the government only aggravated the situation. Given these divergent points of view, the government finds itself in a delicate situation and it must act with great circumspection. I also emphasized the propaganda campaign that the Jews are waging and I said that we must not act on rumours. If anyone has complaints to make, let him inform us and we will go about verifying them. At the same time, I stressed the fact that the government feels very bitter because people are saying that the Synod's requests are falling on deaf ears, even though the Holy Synod has told me more than once that no other minister had been so accommodating of the Synod and its desires (as an example, I cited the way in which the problem of religious education in the high schools had been resolved and the way that the problematic situation of professors teaching religion had been arranged; I also cited the exemption of religious offices from taxes, which used to go into the state coffers, as well as the settlement of the problem of compensation for the metropolitans, etc.). The king was of the same opinion, and he stressed that he could not hide the pain that Neofit's letter had caused him; Neofit objected, saying that the views expressed in the letter were not his own but those of the Synod. Generally speaking, we took an aggressive stance on the Jewish question and the metropolitans found themselves on the defensive . . .

26 May. Wednesday. From six to seven-thirty at Moskovska Street, at the king's. He totally approves of the measures against the Jews . . .

6

Charles Rédard's Report to the Federal Political Department in Berne

11 March 1943

Acting on instructions from the foreign interests section, I urged the Bulgarian government to suspend the deportation of the Jews, if it is still planned, so as to permit the British government to increase as much as possible the number of Bulgarian Jews admitted to Palestine. About a week ago, a brutal invasion was carried out in Thrace and Macedonia, resulting in a round-up of all the Jews from these regions and their transfer to concentration camps in the interior of the country. They number about 12,000.

This morning, I met with Prime Minister Filov. After I explained the problem to him and respectfully urged him to have the children assembled in Sofia so that they could be sent ahead to Palestine, I appealed to his sense of humanity and asked him to halt the deportation of these Jews to Poland where they are being sent to their death.

This was the first time, in all my meetings with the Bulgarian government, that I observed so curt and strong a reaction, even though Mr Filov is the most courteous and agreeable of men:

'How can you speak of a sense of humanity when cities with no military importance, no barracks or even factories of military importance are being bombed? The measures that the Bulgarian government has been forced to take, and has no intention to cancel now, have been dictated by these circumstances.

'One cannot speak of a sense of humanity when our enemies' planes are blindly killing women and children, sowing death and destruction. We are forced to wage a total war: we will either win or die. Germany and Bulgaria are lacking in manpower. We will take it wherever we can find it. By their behaviour the Jews have proven themselves hostile to the interests of the Bulgarian state. They would pose a grave danger if Bulgaria became a theatre of military operations. No one knows what the future may bring. It is possible that a second front, of which there has been so much talk, will not open up in the Balkans, but there are no guarantees that this danger will never arise. We must take precautions. That is why, to my regret, I cannot satisfy your request: the Jews evacuated from Thrace and Macedonia will be sent to Poland where they will work either in factories or in the Todt organizations. The government has made no decision as yet concerning the Jews living within Bulgaria's former borders, but I cannot assure you that such a decision will never be made. We will determine which Jews will be allowed to leave for Palestine, which ones will remain here, and which ones will be sent to the General Government.* The Jews who remain in Bulgaria will be mobilized and will work in organizations similar to the Todt† organizations in Germany.

'I have nothing more to say about this matter. You yourself know that we have tried until now to allow everyone his freedom, this freedom that Bulgarians so cherish. But we are now experiencing a time when state interests take precedence over everything else, when the government has the obligation to safeguard the security of the entire nation. I am the first to

---

*The part of Poland annexed by the Germans.

†The German Todt organizations, named after its founder, built roads and military installations for Germany during World War II, using both slave labour and young people drafted from local populations in Nazi-occupied countries.

regret certain decisions we are forced to make, but I maintain that our treatment of the Bulgarian Jews is more humane than the bombing of civilian populations living peacefully in non-militarized areas.'

Mr Filov added that other countries, like Croatia, Slovakia, and Romania, have taken similar measures; only Italy and Hungary decided to find a different solution to the Jewish question. I pointed out that, to the best of my knowledge, Romania had abandoned its plans to send Jews to Poland. Mr Filov answered that he had received, at the end of last year, information totally to the contrary, according to which there were practically no more Jews left in Romania.

I then urged Mr Filov to tell me whether besides the Jews there were other foreigners living in Bulgaria who would be affected by the deportation. Mr Filov answered that only the Jews would be deported ...

At the end of the meeting, Mr Filov, smiling benevolently once more, left me with the distinct impression that the Bulgarian government would not reconsider its decision concerning the Jews and that it stands firm in its decision to continue, by all the means at its disposal, to support Axis policies and maintain its position as faithful keeper of the Balkan fortress and, if need be, its defender.

Please receive, Mr Federal Counsellor, the assurance of my profound consideration.

Charles Rédard,
Swiss chargé d'affaires

Internment

This section contains documents from the period following the round-ups of March 1943. The first is the minutes of a meeting of Bulgaria's metropolitans, who stood in the front lines of the defence of the Bulgarian Jews. It is followed by a transcript of the king's comments to the Synod, in response to messages they had sent him (Filov's summary of these same comments appears in his diary, in the previous section).

The remaining three texts in this section concern the evacuation and the internment of Sofia's Jews, in May 1943. One of them is a report sent to the king by Mushanov and Stainov, the two most visible opposition deputies, who consistently opposed the government's anti-Jewish policies. The letter that follows, also addressed to the king, originates from the extra-parliamentary (but non-Communist) opposition. The last text, from July 1943, is from the newspaper *Rabotnichesko Delo* (the *Workers' Cause*), the official organ of the Workers' (i.e., Communist) Party.

I

Minutes of a Special Session of the Holy Synod*

2 April 1943

Declaration of the vicar, session chairman

Following the opening of the regular session of the small cabinet of the Holy Synod, the problem of Bulgaria's Jewish minority was immediately examined, along with other questions. The metropolitan of Sofia read his report, in which we learned that the Commissariat for Jewish Questions has begun to deport all Jews and baptized Jews from the new territories of Thrace and Macedonia; they have been transferred to Poland in sealed wagons. The deportation of Jews from Bulgaria was begun as well, but has been provisionally interrupted. I have received delegations of Jews and, especially, baptized Jews; I have also received visits from charitable Bulgarians, all of whom begged the Church to express its point of view on this question and take up the Jews' defence. The Holy Synod has examined the problem and has undertaken new measures. I personally conveyed a statement to the prime minister on this question . . .

These, then, are the two problems (that of the Jews and that of the structure and direction of our Church) which have forced us to call a special plenary session of the Holy Synod. I ask that the situation of the Jews in our country, converted or otherwise, be examined today, and that afterward the second problem, that of the Curia, be placed on the agenda.

*The Synod consists of the country's eleven metropolitans (or bishops). Its president (or vicar) at the time was Neofit, from the Vidin district.

Cyril, metropolitan of Plovdiv*

I have told the metropolitans in the small cabinet of the Holy Synod what is happening with the deportation of the Jews of Plovdiv. I will mention a few facts here as well. On the night of 9 March, at 3:00 a.m., between 1500 and 1600 Jews were arrested in Plovdiv. They were assembled in a schoolhouse and were to be sent to Poland, like the Jews from the new territories of Thrace and Macedonia. I learned of this later in the day. I did not know exactly what was happening and assumed that Jews all over the country had been arrested overnight. A special train was supposed to arrive at the station to take them away. There was widespread indignation among the public.

All I could do was act in accordance with the decisions and instructions of the Holy Synod and follow the voice of my conscience. I sent a telegram to His Majesty the King, begging him in God's name to have pity on these unfortunate people. I then asked to speak with the chief of police who was in Plovdiv that day but I was not able to make contact with him. I tried to find the district police chief, but I was told that he, too, was unavailable. I then decided to call his assistant and I politely urged him to let the government know that I, who until now have always been loyal towards the government, now reserved the right to act with a free hand in this matter and heed only the dictates of my conscience.

Then I received the delegation of baptized Jews. I calmed them, telling them that if they were in danger, they could take asylum in my house. Now we will see whether [the authorities] will come to seek them there. In acting thus, I was following the example of the first Christians, who not only rescued their

*Cyril (1901–71), metropolitan of Plovdiv, the country's second-largest city, would subsequently become metropolitan of Sofia and First Patriarch of the Bulgarian Orthodox Church (1953–71).

own but also took up collections among themselves to buy the freedom of foreign-born Christian slaves. I was informed subsequently that an order had been given, around noon, to free the prisoners; it was received with great joy. To their credit, the Plovdiv police behaved well towards the prisoners.

Stefan, metropolitan of Sofia*

Our brothers know that the bulk of Bulgaria's Jewish minority lives in Sofia or within the confines of the Sofia diocese – Dupnitsa, Kyustendil, Samokov, etc. These Jews fall into two categories: the baptized and the others. Among the former, some were baptized before the promulgation of the Law for the Defence of the Nation, others at the time of its promulgation, and still others afterwards. As of today, I have received some 150 requests, which will be examined when the Holy Synod has clarified the problem. I have had many occasions to witness the suffering of these poor people. On a single day, I received four delegations. That was at the beginning of February, when the Brannik† declared a pogrom against the Jews. Young members of this organization brutalized Jews in the street, tearing the yellow star from their jackets, and then accusing them of not wearing it. There were many wounded and some deaths. One delegation was composed of mothers who begged me to intercede to guarantee the freedom of our fellow citizens, especially the children. There was nothing I could do other than to urge the competent authorities to show some pity and humanity. The second delegation was from the Jewish community, the third

---

*Stefan (1878–1957), who had served as metropolitan bishop of Sofia since 1921, became an exarch in 1945 but was deposed in 1948 and interned in a village until the end of his life. See p. 125.

†The Brannik (Defenders) were, along with the Legionnaires and the Ratnik (Guardians), another group of the Bulgarian extreme right.

was composed of baptized Jews, and the fourth of individuals in mixed marriages.

What helped me considerably in my attempts to reassure the frightened Jews was the intervention of the esteemed Mrs Karavelova.* She worked very hard to put a halt to the Brannik's exactions. The police also intervened to bring an end to this pogrom. But hardly had these persecutions begun to abate than the rumour began to circulate that the Jews were being taken to concentration camps. Again, people became anxious and visits from the delegations resumed. At this time, around 28 February, I was travelling in the environs of Dupnitsa. Some prominent Christians came to see me. Deeply troubled, they informed me that their Jewish fellow citizens had been arrested and were being held under extremely harsh conditions. They told me that a camp had been set up for the Macedonian and Thracian Jews. I said that the Jews had to be treated with leniency, and other high-profile personalities intervened as well. This massive intervention helped to free Dupnitsa's Jews. As for the Thracian and Macedonian Jews, as they are foreigners and not our fellow citizens, all attempts to intervene have proven unsuccessful. People have described terrifying and heart-rending scenes and told me of the horrible conditions under which the Jews are being held. The compassionate people of Dupnitsa begged me, on my return to Sofia, to intercede in favour of the Jews who had been deported to the camps and, according to eyewitnesses, were being treated with inhuman cruelty. But once again my efforts came to naught and, shortly afterwards, the deportees were transported to the Danube ports.

These facts drove me to send a third report to the Holy

*Ekaterina Karavelova, widow of ex-Prime Minister Petko Karavelov, enjoyed considerable prestige in the country. She also interceded directly with the king on behalf of the Jews.

Synod and to urge it, as supreme religious authority, to intercede in favour of the Jews in general and the baptized Jews in particular. The Jews know well that there is no one to speak for them with authority except for the Bulgarian Church, and that if she acts forcefully, her voice will be heard. Our protection is especially needed by the baptized Jews, who must feel that they are accepted and treated as true children of the Holy Church. Unfortunately, the Law for the Defence of the Nation is being implemented by a man who, I am told, lacks the requisite objectivity to deal with these matters. If our Church does not intervene, we should expect even worse outrages and acts of cruelty, which our people, who are good and kind, will one day recall in shame, and perhaps other calamities . . .

2

Protocol No. 9, 6 June 1943, on King Boris's Speech to the Small Cabinet of the Holy Synod

Meeting of 15 April 1943

'... The reason [for this meeting],' [the king] said, 'is indeed the letter from His Eminence the Grand Vicar and chairman of the Holy Synod, accompanied by a letter from the entire Synod and by a proposal to amend certain articles in the Rules of the Exarchate pertaining to the election of the chairman of the Curia. If I did not know His Eminence as well as I do, this letter might have pained me. But I have long been aware of his benevolent feelings towards me and his ecclesiastical zeal. That is why I accord all due respect to the ideas presented in his letter which clarify the matters also contained in the Holy Synod's exposition. It is for these reasons that I thought it appropriate to assemble the directors of the supreme power of the state as well as those of the Church so that these problems can be debated and further clarified. I will begin with a few words on the first problem treated in that letter, that of the Jews.'

And His Majesty began with these 'few words' which lasted more than a half-hour ... He emphasized, in his speech, the enormous harm inflicted on humanity for centuries by the profiteering spirit of the Jews. This spirit has created hatred, loss of faith, moral degeneracy, and treason among men everywhere. This spirit of profiteering and negation has created and still creates discontent, quarrels, conflicts, wars, and calamities among peoples and societies. The present global cataclysm is in large measure the fruit of this profiteering spirit. It is true that some great powers have been able to turn to their own advantage the wealth that the Jews have accumulated thanks to this profiteering spirit. But other European nations have been convinced that Jewish profiteering has been a fatal obstacle to their spiritual, cultural, national, and economic development. These peoples are mature enough to understand that the sooner they rid themselves of Jewish influence and exploitation, the sooner they will be able to strengthen and consolidate their sense of nationhood and their patriotism. This objective cannot be attained unless the various economic, financial, commercial, and industrial enterprises held by the Jews are taken, by law, from Jewish hands. Throughout Europe, legislation to this effect has been enacted and is being enacted still. Here in our country as well, such a legislation has been enacted – the Law for the Defence of the Nation. Our Orthodox Church, known for its patriotism, cannot in this instance hold a contrary opinion.

The meeting was adjourned, due to the lateness of the hour.

[Signed by the members of the Holy Synod]

3

Letter from Nikola Mushanov and Petko Stainov to King Boris

24 May 1943

Your Majesty,

Yesterday, something happened to alarm Bulgarian society: the authorities gave written instructions to a large number of Bulgarians of Jewish origin, ordering them to leave the capital within three days with their wives and children, taking only limited baggage, their destination being towns in the provinces.

These measures are affecting women, widows, families with young children, helpless old people, Bulgarian citizens, commissioned and non-commissioned officers of the military reserve who have been decorated for their bravery and who deserve well of their country for their undeniable devotion to its interests. The order has caused consternation and indignation within wide circles of Bulgarian society. It came so suddenly and during the holidays, giving the Jews little time to prepare. They have been told which trains will transport them, have had their bread coupons taken from them, and are being sent to cities that are not prepared to receive so many people.

Today we appeared before the prime minister, Mr Filov, and, as members of the National Assembly, we pleaded with him to rescind these cruel measures against our fellow citizens of Jewish origin. In spite of all our insistence, in spite of all our arguments proving the illegality and unconstitutionality of these measures and the harm that they will cause the state, he refused to cancel them or even defer their implementation.

In view of this, we beg you to take under your high protection these people who are your subjects and our fellow citizens, so that they will not be exposed to these cruel measures that stain Bulgaria's reputation and are harmful to our interests.

We beg Your Majesty to receive the expression of our devotion.

Nikola Mushanov, deputy from the
Second Electoral College of Sofia
Professor Petko Stainov, deputy from the
First Electoral College of Kazanlâk

4

Letter from Public Figures* to King Boris

26 May 1943

Your Majesty,

Two days ago, the Commissariat for Jewish Questions ordered residents of Sofia who are of Jewish origin to prepare their most essential personal effects, to draw up and submit an inventory of their personal property, and to present themselves, together with their families, in three days at specified hours at Sofia station; from there they are to be sent to a destination of unknown origin where they face possible execution.

This mass deportation of Bulgarian citizens who enjoy the same rights as all others and who are guilty of no crime has been condemned by the great majority of Bulgarians and aroused their compassion. In subjecting our innocent fellow citizens to this cruel and pitiless measure, not only are we squandering a vast moral capital of which our generous and tolerant people had every right to be proud, we are also harming Bulgaria's reputation in the eyes of the world and compromising its future national interests.

Only Your Majesty can cancel this inhuman measure which so ill befits the spirit of our peace-loving people, because Your Majesty is the embodiment of our government. Otherwise,

*This letter was drafted by two politicians, Tsvyatko Boboshevski and Damyan Velchev, members of the extra-parliamentary non-Communist opposition. It was co-signed by a number of other public figures of the same tendency, such as D. Kazasov, N. Mushanov, K. Pastukhov, N. Petkov, etc.

Your Majesty will bear full responsibility. We believe it our most urgent duty to draw Your Majesty's attention to the preparations being made against our Jewish compatriots, who, like the Jews from Thrace and Macedonia, are to be deported, even though they have committed no crime. We are convinced that Your Majesty will not fail to stop these fatal measures. Heeding our warning, Your Majesty will abrogate this order.

5

'Mad Assault against the Jews': An Article from the *Workers' Cause**

July 1943

The deportation of Sofia's Jewish population is almost over. More than 50,000 Jewish residents, born and brought up in Sofia, were forced to abandon their homes, property, and jobs, and leave Sofia for various parts of the country;[†] then, divided into small groups, separated and disarmed, they were chased to the borders of Bulgaria and sent to Poland, that terrifying graveyard for Jews, or elsewhere, to some hellish fascist labour camp.

All last month, residents of Sofia witnessed cruelties worthy of fascist barbarians. Policemen and Branniks made the rounds of Jewish neighbourhoods, delivering the deadly deportation orders. The Jews, a peaceful and mainly proletarian population, had to leave Sofia in three days without even having time to sell their belongings and household goods or being allowed to take with them their least personal belongings, necessary to life.

Sofia was horrified. The harrowing scenes witnessed these past days will not be forgotten for years to come. Knowing full well what the deportation means, people preferred to die in their homes rather than be herded like cattle to the slaughter-house. One father shot his wife and his two children before

---

*This clandestine newspaper was the organ of the Bulgarian Workers' Party (the Communist Party).

†The total number of Bulgarian Jews at the time was about 48,000. About 25,000 lived in Sofia; close to 20,000 were expelled from the city.

taking his own life; a mother killed her infant child by throwing it out of the window and then poisoned herself. These incidents are not the exception. Heart-rending cries were heard from every Jewish home. Furniture and household goods were piled up in the streets, a makeshift marketplace for these suffering people. With tears in their eyes, they parted from everything they had accumulated with their hard labour.

On 24 May, more than 10,000 Jews* went out into the streets of Sofia to defend their right to live. Women with children in their arms stood at the head of the demonstration. They went to ask to be left to live, work, and die in their country. But against this deeply righteous action, the government, which has sold out to Hitler, sent the police. The raving police hordes rushed from all sides upon the Jewish mass. These rabid dogs stampeded cruelly over children, elderly people, and pregnant women. They turned the Jewish quarter into a real battlefield. Hundreds of policemen armed with machine guns and automatic rifles took over the school. Like a pack of wolves, they broke into houses, beat the women and children, arrested the men.

Thus the day of the great teachers of the Slavs, Cyril and Methodius, a day when the Bulgarians for centuries have demonstrated their love for freedom, fraternity among peoples, and national awakening†, was turned by the fascist obscurantists into a day of shame and tears. This ugly crime could not but disgust every honourable Bulgarian. The honest true Bulgarian felt ashamed that, in our country, the country of Botev, Levski, and Karadja,‡ such acts could be committed,

*This figure is disputed. Other eyewitnesses speak of 1500 demonstrators, mainly Jews.

† 24 May is celebrated in Bulgaria as Cyril and Methodius' Day, honouring these two 'evangelists of the Slavs' who are regarded as pioneers of Bulgarian culture. Every Bulgarian city typically holds a parade of schoolchildren on this day.

‡These are the heroes of the struggle for freedom from Turkish rule in the nineteenth century.

that here too, in Bulgaria, fascism could have brought up such beasts who delighted in the suffering of others and whose hearts did not respond to the tears of mothers, nor to the cries of children . . .

King Boris and the Filov cabinet sold out the independence of the country, turned it into an enslaved hungry land, stained it with the blood of the best and most worthy sons of the people, committed more than one crime against our neighbouring and fraternal peoples, the Yugoslavs and the Greeks, and now in their criminal recklessness, they are driving our country to the abyss that gapes pitilessly under the feet of Hitler and his allies. For all these crimes the government and the king have earned the anger and hatred of the Bulgarian people. In their treacherous policy, they are alone with their horrible clique, and the people have turned their backs on them. That is why they are looking for a means to divert the attention of the people's masses and direct their anger away from themselves. This is the crux of the matter and the reason for the shameless persecution of the Jews. They want to blame the Jews for all the misfortunes and difficulties that the Bulgarian people are going through as a result of the treacherous policy of the government.

The Jews provoked the war, the Jews are to blame for the high prices, the Jews were to blame for the profiteering that overruns our entire economic life, etc. etc.

Yet who would believe that the poor pedlars selling safety pins and shoelaces, the cabbies and porters from Trapezitsa Square and Serdika Street, the elderly people, tired from life, who quietly smoke their tobacco along the pavements of Positano Street, the thousands of Jewish women and children – who would believe that they are to blame for today's bloody fascist butchery? Who will believe that these people, steeped in poverty, are to blame for the high prices today? Who does not know that high prices came to this country together with the hungry Germans? Prices soared and reached terrifying heights when all food and other goods began to be exported to Germany and our market was flooded with worthless bills. The entire Bulgarian people also knows that the ministers and their friends took advantage of the war and with the help of profiteering and the black market, they accumulated vast fortunes . . .

Bulgarian citizens and public figures, silent dissatisfaction and quiet protest are not enough. Fascist tyranny cannot be crushed by them nor our people be salvaged from hunger, robbery, and terror. It is necessary that all forces join the people's liberation movement. The place of every honest Bulgarian and public figure is in the ranks of the struggle under the banner of the Fatherland Front.

It is the patriotic duty of every Bulgarian to unite in a powerful campaign in defence of the Jews, which will embrace all democratic and patriotic forces in this country and prevent the materialization of the intentions of the king, the government, and the remaining agents of Hitler in this country, grouped around the well-known assassins, Tsankov and Jekov.*

We warn you that the problem of the deportation of the Jews from the country is not precluded. The government was obliged to put it off for the time being, but, under favourable circumstances, it will try to fulfil its criminal intentions. The latter can be prevented only with a consistent, bold, and persistent struggle. Society and the Jews must be on the alert . . .!

With joint efforts and decisive actions, the fascist beast will be crushed.

*General Nikola Jekov and Professor Alexander Tsankov (1879–1959) were two politicians of the extreme right. In spite of his participation in the rightist opposition, Tsankov nevertheless co-signed Peshev's protest letter (see p. 78).

MEMOIRS

The documents translated here are of an entirely different nature from those preceding them; written after the fact, they look back on the events from the distance of time.

Dimo Kazasov's memoirs are the only ones to have been published in Bulgaria before 1989; one can sense this in their style. Kazasov (1886–1980) had a long political career before 1944, but following the *coup d'état*, he lent his services to the Communist powers. The excerpts from Kazasov's memoirs that follow are drawn from various sources: *Prezhivelici*, Sofia, Ot. front, 1979, pp. 128–9 in the case of the first, dated 1935; *Vidjano i prezhivjano*, Sofia, Ot. front, 1969, pp. 612–15, in the case of the second, dated 1940; and *Iskri ot burni godini*, Sofia, Ot. front, 1987, pp. 181–3 in the case of the last, dated 1943.

The other texts did not emerge from the archives until after the fall of Communism in 1989. Stefan, exarch of Bulgaria between 1945 and 1948, suffered a stormy fate, in many ways not unlike that of the people he defended during the war: his independent spirit earned him dismissal from his post, deportation, and internment in the village of Banya. He wrote his memoirs in 1950; the excerpts published here first appeared in the compilation *Oceljavaneto*.

The episode in which Peshev figures so prominently appears in several published memoirs, notably those of National Assembly deputy Petâr Mikhalev, written in 1973, and the 1976 memoirs of the businessman Asen Suichmezov, a member of the delegation from Kyustendil, which travelled to Sofia in March 1943. Excerpts from Suichmezov's memoirs appear here in translation.

The memoirs of Peshev himself were written at the suggestion of a sympathetic staff member at the State Archives in Sofia, between 1969 and 1970. They were deposited in the Archives, with the exception of one notebook concerning his experience with the People's Tribunal between 1944 and 1945; that notebook remains in his family's possession and unfortunately is still inaccessible to scholars. Peshev thus intended his text not for publication but for history; the freedom he demonstrates in his judgments reflects this. The pages devoted to the persecution of the Jews form but a small part of what was deposited with the Archives; they appear here in their entirety. Peshev first describes the place of the Jewish community in Bulgaria's economic life prior to the war and retraces the history of the first persecutions, before turning to the episode in which he was personally involved.

The subdivisions in his text have been introduced by me.

Dimo Kazasov, Petâr Mikhalev, Dimitâr Peshev, and Asen Suichmezov are among the thirteen 'righteous' Bulgarian Jews honoured in Israel at Yad Vashem.

I

Dimo Kazasov

[1935]

Having won the elections through violence and fraud, Hitler had to rule by terror if he was to stay in power. The concentration camps that were set up in Dachau, Auschwitz, Majdanek, Buchenwald, and Mauthausen, are his creation. One of the first camps was Dachau, not far from Munich, some two kilometres from the village of Dachau. Opened in 1934, this graveyard contained a crematorium and operating rooms for dangerous and deadly medical experimentation.

As part of a group of Bulgarian journalists who had arrived in Munich, I was taken to Dachau along with my colleagues, so that we might observe the good and humane conditions under which the 'criminals' who were dangerous to the state were being held.

We stopped before the camp gate, the single opening in the barbed-wire fence that ringed the compound. Two soldiers armed with automatic rifles stood guard. Above the gate a platform had been erected, on which one could make out the muzzles of two machine guns, with a sentry standing beside them. Binoculars hung from the neck of the guards. One of the guards pushed the button of a buzzer behind him. Instantly, a man in uniform appeared; our guard exchanged a few words with him and then disappeared. We waited. After fifteen minutes or so, the camp director stood before us, his hand raised in the fascist salute. We followed him.

We passed through a large, bright, and well-equipped

carpentry workshop where many prisoners dressed in smocks could be seen at work. As we walked by the men, not one of them would even look up at us. It was obvious! This was a silent protest against the curiosity of people who, from their perspective, could only be Nazis. From the workshop we entered a spacious courtyard filled with small huts, their doors wide open. We stole a glance into one of them. There were two pallets, one above the other. Right next to the lower one stood a small and narrow table, about the length of the bunks. Not a single chair. We realized that what was being used as a chair was the lower bunk, where one could not sit and keep one's back straight at the same time. On the table there were two photos. One was a portrait of a man and several young women; the other was of an elderly couple with two little boys of school age. That was all. Two small objects in which great pain and small consolation were concentrated.

A long bell brought us out from this human tragedy hidden away inside the little hut. It was noon and, from all sides, people in work smocks poured from the buildings and made their way toward the centre of the immense courtyard. They lined up in rows and waited. Soon, an officer arrived: he stood at attention before the rows of workers, his hand raised. A clamour rent the air, to the sound of 'Heil Hitler!' The victims were saluting their tormentor. At the officer's signal, an orchestra began to play the Hitlerian march. Then all of them hurried off to the mess hall, which we were not shown. Nor were we shown any of the other workshops. On our way out of the camp, as we walked alongside the barbed wire, our guide warned us not to come too close, because an electric current ran through it day and night.

That was all we saw of Dachau. There were also gas chambers and medical experiments there, and stone isolation cells where neither air nor a single ray of sunlight could penetrate.

Our group included people of the most varied political opinions, but I can say with certainty that we all left Dachau profoundly shaken . . .

[1940]

On 14 September, another *coup d'état* took place in Romania, instigated by the German fifth column. The Iron Guard, following the example of the Nazi Party, declared itself the national party, and its leader, Chorea Sima, became vice-chairman of the Council of Ministers. Not to be outdone by its Romanian partners in this display of loyalty to Hitler, the Bulgarian government made public the proposed Law for the Defence of the Nation. Drafted by the minister of internal affairs, it was a law that, in essence, proposed to outlaw the Jews.

The bill met with violent resistance from the Bulgarian people, whose spirit of tolerance could not silently accept the anti-Semitism that the new Bulgarian racists were trying to graft onto a land watered with the blood of thousands of men and women who had fought for complete equality among peoples. The Bulgarians knew full well what it meant to be enslaved, oppressed, and denied all rights; they could not wish these oppressive social conditions on others or remain indifferent to this shameful law that put a stain on our history, our traditions, and our struggles. And so with protests and petitions the people rose up against the cannibalism of the Nazi campaign. The intelligentsia acquitted itself honourably of its duty as well, not hesitating for a moment, despite censorship and legal measures, to speak out in condemnation of the government's anti-Semitic campaign. In spite of these protests, in spite of the Bulgarian people's open rejection of the draft bill, it was introduced on 6 November [15 November in the Gregorian calendar] into the National Assembly.

The feelings excited by this law were not only a reaction to anti-Semitism; they were also a reaction to the division of the world into two opposing camps – the democratic camp, and the fascist camp. Examining the points of view expressed on this law allows one to better discern how the Bulgarian people situated themselves with respect to these two camps. The social strata that were openly opposed to the law included the workers, peasants, tradesmen, the progressive sector of the commercial and industrial bourgeoisie, the Church, and the intelligentsia. The social strata who supported it were the predatory commercial and industrial bourgeoisie, the vindictive Germanophile intelligentsia, and the lumpen proletariat.

Politically speaking, members of the old parties associated with the government were in favour of the law: the Tsankovite movement,* the national liberals, and all the other various and sundry nationalist and fascist groups. On the other side, opposing the law, were the Communist Party and all the parties of the left, as well as the populists and the democrats.

Government censorship made it impossible for the people and the progressive forces to express their opposition to the bill publicly. As a citizen with no party affiliation, I allowed myself, as soon as this legislative project surfaced, to circulate an open letter that I had written to the prime minister and the deputies, in which I attacked the government's measure† ...

A few prominent writers, led by Elin-Pelin, also signed a petition against the law. The Bulgarian Orthodox Church, under the aegis of the Synod, condemned this bill, which was modelled after German legislation.

The debates over the measure in the National Assembly were heated.

*The Tsankovite Movement was a prominent right-wing political force in Bulgaria until 1935.
†The text of this letter appears on p. 58.

In 1937 in Sofia, a book, *Bulgarian Public Opinion and the Problems of Racism and Anti-Semitism*, was brought out. In it, fifty-seven public figures, including politicians, scholars, writers, journalists, actors, and painters, spoke out openly and clearly against the Nazi-inspired anti-Semitic campaign. Among the names of these fifty-seven citizens was that of Alexander Tsankov, who declared, albeit timidly, his opposition to the persecution of the Jews. He said, 'We are following the example of our Lord Jesus Christ: [let there be] neither vengeance nor violence but only feelings of brotherhood for those who, like any other Bulgarian citizens, can have whatever religion they choose.'

Once the measure was put before the National Assembly, however, Tsankov chose to remain silent; and when a deputy from the government majority made some insinuating comment about Tsankov's position, Tsankov replied, 'In principle, I am in favour of a law for the defence of the Bulgarian nation against those elements whose race makes them foreign to us. I have voted for the law.'

The German storm was now raging in every corner of our country and Tsankov was eager to distance himself from anything that might suggest that he had taken a stand against it.

On 20 November, the law was voted in, and this was further proof that Boris III had decided which camp our country would join.

Over the next three years, the Law for the Defence of the Nation underwent a series of amendments authorizing confiscation of property belonging to Jews and taking away their rights. They had to wear the yellow star on their lapels and post it on their houses.

But Hitler's minions were still not satisfied. They passed a bill giving the government unrestricted powers to take whatever anti-Jewish measures it deemed necessary . . .

[1943]

Hitler succeeded in having the Jews deported from Yugoslavia, Greece, and Romania, and burned in the ovens of Auschwitz and Majdanek. Of all the Jewish communities in the Balkans, only Bulgaria's escaped unscathed. It was rescued by the silent but steadfast resistance of the Bulgarian people. In a thousand different ways, they let the government know that they would not permit it to consign to a cruel fate people who had lived with them in peace and mutual understanding for almost five centuries [since 1492, when the Jews were expelled from Spain] and who, for the most part, had helped them in their struggle for independence.

Caught between pressure from Hitler and opposition from the people, the government took the path of least resistance: it turned its attack on the Jews from the occupied territories, where the Communist Party and other progressive forces were not predominant. The cabinet issued the following decree:

'In view of Article 1 of the law empowering the Council of Ministers to take all necessary measures concerning the Jewish question and other related matters, the following decision has been approved: the Commissariat for Jewish Questions is instructed to deport from the country, in concert with the German authorities, 20,000 Jewish persons residing in the recently liberated territories.'

In one tragic night, the Jews from Thrace and Macedonia were taken from their homes and sent without baggage or money to Dupnitsa and Gorna Djumaya, where they were transferred to sealed wagons and transported to the port of Lom. From there, they were sent up the Danube and transported via Vienna to Poland, where, in the skies above villages drowning in sorrow, winds dispersed the ashes of their countrymen.

The reaction of the Bulgarian people in the face of this act of barbarity was so overwhelming that it was able to rouse the conscience of a number of deputies in the National Assembly. Forty-two of them, led by the vice-chairman of the National Assembly, Dimitâr Peshev, addressed a protest letter to the government demanding a halt to this cruelty.

Not only did this action fail to dissuade the government from its evil undertaking, it in fact aroused the government's ire. The government demanded that the vice-chairman of the National Assembly and main signatory to the letter be censured. The vote of censure took place under scandalous conditions: it was never properly entered into the legislative agenda, there was no debate, and Peshev was not allowed to speak in his own defence.

No one can describe the terror felt by the Jews from the new territories as they waited to be deported. Parents, loved ones, and friends wept bitter tears as they ran from house to house to say goodbye for the last time. Mothers and fathers, sons and daughters, brothers and sisters, stood for hours locked in one another's embrace until finally, racked with sobs, they had to separate; they left, then looked behind them and turned back, throwing themselves one last time into the arms of those from whom cruelty would separate them for ever. Little children stood frozen before these scenes, uncomprehending of the tragedy raging around them.

The path from the prison cell to the gallows is short, but it is filled with infinite terror. What dread, then, must lie scattered along the thousands of kilometres of roads and rails connecting [the Jews'] native towns and villages to Auschwitz. Before the eyes of the 'deported' Jews, endless processions passed by – men, women, and children whom the monstrous barbarity of Hitlerism dragged towards the tomb with stony indifference. To travel for days and nights, to see life teeming all around you at every port and every station, in the fields and along the roads, and to know, as you hurtle along these sun-soaked roads, that you already wear the terrifying mask of death; to know that you are not alone in this fatal journey but that those nearest and dearest to you have been condemned as well; to look towards the far-off horizon and see the smoke rising from the crematoria, carrying with it those whom the ovens have turned to fiery cinders; to smell in the air the reek of burnt flesh and hear resounding in your ears the shrill cries of their suffering that shake even the earth beneath the rails; and to know that soon you too, and all those with you on that train, will be no more than a fistful of hot ashes, a wisp of smoke carrying your cries skyward in the suffocating silence of the night; to see and to know that all this is your ineluctable fate is truly a thousand times more terrible than death.

2

Metropolitan Stefan

Banya, Karlovo District, 17 October 1950

As metropolitan of Sofia, the diocese where there lived the greatest number of Jews during those tragic times, we stood resolutely beside the cruelly persecuted Jewish community, heeding only the voice of our conscience as prescribed by our faith and the obligations imposed by our civic freedom. Acting from our position of authority within the Church, we addressed many messages to the public, to the government, and to our head of state, urging that the deportation of the Jews to Poland be stopped and that those who had already been deported to the concentration camps be returned to their homes. We wanted our appeal to carry the weight of the entire Bulgarian Orthodox Church, and so we presented several statements to the Holy Synod (the supreme religious authority in our country) authorizing it to intercede with the king to bring about the cancellation of the law against our country's Jewish minority. This intercession was pursued with obstinacy and fervour; we did not hide the fact that the law was subjecting Jews to terror and pillage.

The intercession of Holy Synod did not achieve its objective and the anti-Jewish measures remained in force; it did, however, help mitigate the implementation of the Nazi measures and postpone the decision to deport massive numbers of Jews to Poland . . .

In the spring of 1943, on our way to the holy monastery of Rila, we were stopped at a train crossing on the road from

Dupnitsa to Kocherinovo, and watched as a train carrying Jews from Thrace and Kavala passed by. What I saw exceeded my notions of horror and my conception of inhumanity. In the freight wagons, there were old and young, sick and well, mothers with their nursing babies, pregnant women, packed like sardines and weak from standing; they cried out desperately for help, for pity, for water, for air, for a scrap of humanity ... The train was guarded by Nazis, the wagons were sealed; it was headed for the Danube, and the final destination was Poland. Profoundly distressed by what we had seen, we continued on to the holy cloister, where we sent a telegram to the head of state, begging him to take action so that the Jews expelled from Thrace could travel across Bulgaria like human beings, not like cattle, and to alleviate their intolerable conditions; at the same time, we expressed our wish that they not be sent to Poland, a name that had a sinister ring, even to the ears of babies.

In answer to our telegram, we received a message, informing us that everything possible and legal would be done ...

By some unfortunate and inexplicable coincidence, the most tragic day for Bulgaria's Jews was the day of Bulgarian culture, that great holiday of the two brother apostles Cyril and Methodius. It had been decided that on that very day, a major round-up of Jews throughout Bulgaria would begin, and it was conducted with particular cruelty in Sofia, our capital. We were preparing for the solemn celebration that was about to take place on the stately Saint Alexander Nevski Square which was filled with students and city residents. As we were leaving our residence, we were taken aback by an enormous wave of men, women, and youths of Jewish origin, all wearing the yellow star, who had come to inform us of the persecutions and arrests that had been going on since dawn. We went back into the house and received in our office a delegation headed by the Chief Rabbi, Dr Hananel, and by the venerable rabbi

[Tsion], who gave us a brief but eloquent and cogent report on what was happening that day to the Jews in Bulgaria, particularly in Sofia. The distress and pain that could be read on their faces, caused by this cruel pogrom that had been started precisely on this our country's finest day, a day respected and celebrated by Jews and Bulgarians alike, brought tears to my eyes.

We used the little time available to us to contact the palace, in order to protest against this barbarity and urge that it be stopped without delay. At the palace, they told us the king had left Sofia. We then tried to reach the chief of his inner cabinet, Mr P. Gruev, which we were in fact able to do. Briefly, we told Mr Gruev of the delegation that had come to see us, of the crowd of Jews that was now in the courtyard and in the street in front of our residence, seeking the aid of our Holy Church, asking for compassion and justice. This, we said, was the motivation behind our decision to urge His Majesty to declare authoritatively and decisively, 'Enough!'

'Convey to His Majesty,' we told Mr Gruev, 'that he should do this for his own sake and defuse the tension that this totally unwarranted persecution has created and that is spoiling today's great holiday. The wails and tears of these Bulgarian citizens of Jewish origin whose rights are being denied them are a legitimate protest against the injustice being done to them, and it is neither possible nor fitting that this protest not be heard and redressed by the king of the Bulgarians, whom we implore, today more than ever before, to demonstrate the compassion and lucidity incumbent on his position by defending the right to the freedom and human dignity that the Bulgarian people have always upheld by tradition and by temperament.' Mr Gruev promised to do whatever he could and suggested that, when the religious services had ended, we intercede in a similar manner with the prime minister who, in this instance, was the more competent authority . . .

We went to Saint Alexander Nevski Cathedral at the appointed hour and celebrated the solemn rite on the vast cathedral square, daring to comment, in our final sermon, that this year our holiday was marred by the pogrom being waged against the Jews, and that today's celebration was an untraditional one, for it lacked the attendance of our studious Jewish youths. This obliged us, we said, to call out to the state authorities from this square and beg them not to shackle the democratic and hospitable spirit characteristic of the Bulgarian people, a spirit forged by humanity and brotherly love, and hostile to foreign influence, foreign control, and foreign demands. Under the great roof of the Church, there were no problems with national minorities, because the Bulgarians were tolerant and their fundamental law was respect for freedom, which overcame the peculiarities of the minorities and the domination of the majority. On this great day on which we celebrated the two holy apostles, we beseeched those who steered the ship of state to put aside all exclusionary, discriminatory, and oppressive policies. It was our duty to prove ourselves worthy of the commandment that, in creating us spiritually, had educated Bulgaria in the gospel's truth, so that she could be, then as now, a state enlightened by the shining beacons of culture and built in a democratic and disciplined spirit.

After the service and the student youth parade that followed, we had a brief conversation with Prime Minister Filov, that, to our sadness and pain, ended in a categorical refusal: 'The law concerning Bulgaria's Jews,' the prime minister said, putting an end to the discussion, 'is a state necessity. As such, it cannot be cancelled; on the contrary, its enforcement will continue.' In finally taking leave of us, he advised us, as a friend, that we should stop bothering His Majesty the King as well as the government with our interventions with regard to the law concerning the Jews . . .

In the face of all this – the government's refusal to stop the round-ups of the Jews; the inability of the king's adviser, Mr Gruev, to contact His Majesty; our realization that a large number of those who had come to see us that very morning had been arrested and were now being held in police gaols while awaiting transfer to the concentration centres; the possibility that they would be expelled from Bulgaria; the news that even the rabbis had been arrested – we decided, with great distress, to take three measures, [including] a detailed report to His Majesty on the situation of the Jewish minority in our country and an argument explaining why he should exercise his royal authority to put an end to this barbarity, a true indignity to the Bulgarians' peaceful and generous character . . .

In our report, we told His Majesty of our deep sorrow that the feast of the two apostles Cyril and Methodius had been marred by the raids against the Jews and begged his indulgence for having disturbed him of late and for having been so bold as to send him the attached report in order to draw his attention to the international as well as domestic complexities of the Jewish problem.

Our report drew on a number of essential principles – Christian (the religious and ethical precept of loving one's neighbour), as well as social and political, financial and economic, altruistic and utilitarian, nationalist and statist (patriotic and democratic) . . .

We concluded our report with these words: 'In keeping with the commandment of the Saviour to love one another, a commandment on which the Church of Christ has been built and in the spirit of which the Bulgarian people have been educated; in keeping with the considerations and prescriptions dictated by international norms for human life; on the basis of aspirations for social justice; in keeping with the real, well-known and deep-felt tolerance that the Bulgarian people have demonstrated with regard to the Jewish minority historically and still demonstrate today, we implore Your Majesty to stop the implementation of the anti-Jewish law and order its full cancellation. Through this august action, Your Majesty, you will dispel the suspicion that Bulgaria is a prisoner of Hitler's anti-European policy, you will spare our country from the greatest crime and most perfidious act – hatred towards men – and you will appear in all the strength and magnificence of your royal power as the protector and defender of the Bulgarian aspiration to liberty and justice, peace and love, thus preserving for evermore the halo of Bulgarian tolerance and democratic spirit . . .'

In response to our report, His Majesty sent his cabinet head to tell us that it had indeed been received and to assure us that the head of state had given it his fullest attention. Just as he had responded favourably to our first appeal, ordering that the Jews exiled from Thrace be well treated in crossing Bulgaria, even though they were prisoners of Hitler's high military command, so in the present situation, His Majesty had taken our request into consideration and seen to it that the treatment of the Jews would be moderated to the fullest extent possible even as the law concerning their future and their rights in our country was carried out. As far as the law itself was concerned, His Majesty wished to remind us that the law had been passed by the government and was the result of our commitments to our allies; in view of this, His Majesty therefore asked that we draw our own conclusions as to its abrogation: could he do it alone? As he was leaving, the head of the king's inner cabinet informed us confidentially that our report had been passed on to the prime minister for his examination . . .

Through the intermediary of his secretary, the prime minister warned us to abandon our effort and let [the Commissariat] carry out its duties. Shortly after receiving this warning, against which we took the liberty of protesting to His Majesty, we were informed, perhaps in response to this protest, that the attorney general was gathering testimony with regard to our defence of the Jews, in view of our being charged with actions harmful to the state. We protested to the head of state but were not favoured with a reply. This was the only case, in all our frequent professional contacts with the king, in which we encountered silence and aloofness; do what we might, the trains rolled on . . .

3

Asen Suichmezov

At the time when pressure on the Jews was intensifying, between 1941 and 1943, I happened to be in Skopje one day, where I saw the sale of personal property belonging to Jews who had been deported to Poland. I was aghast. When I returned to Kyustendil, I was approached by some of the city's Jews who asked me warily whether it were true that soup pots to feed Jews in the camps had already been sent to Kyustendil. Every day, between fifteen and twenty terrified Jews came to ask me this question in confidence. They did not dare come to see me too often for fear that they would be harassed by fascist sympathizers who could easily pick them out by the yellow star they were forced to wear on their lapels. As for myself, the fascists could not stand me, they hated me. I told the frightened Jews that I had seen Jewish property being sold in Skopje but had not heard anything about soup pots being sent here. But during these days, there was no way to reassure them.

One day they came to tell me that they had heard they were soon going to be assembled in the tobacco warehouses and then be deported to Poland, as had been done with the Jews from Thrace and Macedonia. All at once, the Jews began to seek help desperately, begging for delegations to be formed. Forty-four Bulgarians announced that they were ready to join a delegation. The next day, when this delegation was about to leave for Sofia, the assistant chief of police, Miltenov, refused to allow the cars to be fuelled, even though he had promised the day before that they would be. Then I saw the Jews, overcome with despair, going past my workshops, and with tears in their eyes they said to me, 'Goodbye, Asen, we're never going to see you again!' But it so happened that I was one of those who had agreed to be part of the delegation. Momchilov, the lawyer, begged me not to give up as the others had, and he could not stop crying. I told him that I had given my word to the Jews that I would defend them and I would not back out. Jacques Simonet, the French manufacturer, also came to see me, as did other prominent individuals, all with the same objective, that I go to Sofia with the delegation. And that is what I did.

I should say here that even before this time, quite a few fascist sympathizers hated me and threatened me constantly, even as Jews from Kyustendil, Sofia, and Plovdiv kept coming to my workshops to let me know what fate lay in store for them. This attitude earned me a number of public incidents. One evening, Tsindy Kirladjiev and I walked into Georgi 'Truntata' Semerdjiev's tavern; Popov, the waiter, was very hostile to Jews. As soon as he saw me, he grabbed a chair and tried to smash me over the head with it. Kirladjiev came to my defence: he grabbed the chair and did not let Popov strike me. Other people crowded around me and advised me to leave the place: 'Get out of here! You're going to get yourself beaten to death because of these Jews!' We left.

The delegation of forty people that was to leave for Sofia somehow disintegrated. Only four of us remained: Momchilov, the lawyer; Vladimir Kurtev, the schoolteacher; Petâr Mikhalev, the National Assembly deputy, who ended up joining us; and myself. On 8 March 1943, this little delegation left for Sofia, as long lines of freight wagons waited at Kyustendil station, ready for the deportation of the Jews. We arrived in Sofia in the evening and arranged to meet the following morning (9 March 1943), at the corner of Dondukov and Târgovska Streets, at Popov Brothers' hat shop. That morning, as I was getting ready to leave for this appointment, two prominent Jews, the lawyers Jose Pinkas Baruch and his brother Pinkas Baruch, came to see me at my hotel. They immediately begged me to come with them to the Jewish committee which at that very moment was examining the dossiers of Jews who had requested permission to leave for Palestine. And so we went there together. There was a crowd of Jews outside the door, vying with one another for an exit permit, but only a few were supposed to be let inside. It was impossible to get through the door. Yako Barukhov* got the crowd to settle down, the people made way for us, and with great difficulty we managed to squeeze through. I was introduced to the anxious crowd as a member of the delegation from Kyustendil that had come to meet this same day the vice-chairman of the National Assembly, D. Peshev, who would introduce the delegation to the prime minister.

I explained the situation: that we had been given a mandate by the Jews of Kyustendil to urge, in case the deportation was not going to be stopped, that all Jews be assembled in one provincial district or another; after the war, the Bulgarian government could settle matters with them. After this meeting, I went immediately to Popov Brothers', where I found the other members of the delegation, who were waiting for me impatiently. We agreed on a plan of action, and, relying on my personal relations with the vice-chairman of the Assembly, D. Peshev, I managed to reach him by telephone; he immediately invited the delegation to come to his home. To get there as quickly as possible, we took a car to Neofit Rilski Street, where he lived. We explained the reasons for our visit. Peshev and I got into an animated discussion, with each of us completing

*Yako Barukhov (or Baruch) was a prominent socialist and Zionist.

the other's arguments. The atmosphere was tense. I described to him, with tears in my eyes, the tragedy that the Jews of Kyustendil were going through, and I told him about the freight cars that were waiting for them at the station. He immediately replied that the reputation of the Bulgarian people must not be blackened in this way. I made a point of saying that the Jews had begged me to join the delegation. They told me, 'Asen, if you don't go, we're lost!'

We stayed about an hour there with Dimitâr Peshev in his home. Maybe it was the tears that swayed him in the end. In any case, he proposed that we come to see him at the National Assembly at three o'clock in the afternoon. He told us to use the entrance at the back of the building. He would give orders to the guard there to let us in; that way we would not waste time. And in fact he did give the guard a short note: 'A delegation led by Asen Suichmezov will be coming. Have them brought to me.' I forgot to mention that on our way to the National Assembly, Vladimir Kurtev met up with us, to let us know he was about to go and meet Stanishev,* to speak with him too about the problem of the Jews. Therefore he could not come with us, he said, and we must not wait for him. And so it turned out that there would be three of us: Momchilov, Petâr Mikhalev, and myself. At this same time, the prime minister and almost all the ministers were meeting in the cabinet chamber of the National Assembly. Dimitâr Peshev received us in one of the corridors and introduced us to the deputies, with whom we immediately entered into a passionate debate on the Jewish tragedy. Some of them would not hear of anyone's defending the Jews. For them, we were traitors to our country, criminals who had come to stick up for the profiteers, etc.

---

*Alexander Stanishev, a professor of medicine as well as a politician, served as minister of internal affairs and health in the Bagryanov government (June–September 1944). He was executed in 1945.

While we were speaking with the deputies, D. Peshev went to the prime minister, who refused to receive our delegation. So Peshev, together with Mihalev, proceeded to the office of the minister of internal affairs, Gabrovski, and explained his position on our delegation's requests. After some hesitation, Gabrovski telephoned the chief of police and ordered him to stop the deportation of the Jews. At this, Peshev ran out into the corridor and motioned to me to come with him behind the banister, saying, 'Suichmezov, shake my hand: the deportation of the Jews has been stopped, you can phone Kyustendil immediately and tell them the news.' As we left the National Assembly, a large group of Jews was waiting for us at the back door. They had heard the news and they were overjoyed. Buko Leonov, a young Jew from Kyustendil, was beside himself with joy. Shouting through his tears he said, 'God bless you, Asen!' As I was walking to a liquor store to telephone Kyustendil, two men approached me, and the older of them asked which one of us was Asen Suichmezov. I answered that I was. Very moved, he seized my hand and among his words of gratitude, I remember the last ones: 'I have come to shake your hand, I am Colonel Tadjer.* Bravo for your courage!'

Just after my telephone call to Kyustendil, the fascists attacked my house; they smashed the windows, and those at Momchilov's house as well. This happened several times. What with all the tension surrounding these events, I was forced to go into hiding, in Plovdiv, Troyan, Ruse, Sofia, and other cities, where I found refuge with friends . . .

---

*Colonel Avram Tadjer, a veteran of the wars of 1912–13 and 1914–18, and president of the Jewish Consistory after 1920, left the Union of Reserve Officers after the passage of the Law for the Defence of the Nation.

4

Dimitâr Peshev

I feel that I belong to an unfortunate generation that lived through a series of upheavals and saw its most closely held ideals crushed in the end. When I look back on the vicissitudes of the past, its lofty expectations and dark disappointments, I feel the pain of a man who, by dint of pure hopes and great expectations, had reached a bright summit, and then fell from it into an abyss. This sentiment, I believe, is shared by all whose lives, like mine, were ruled by the powerful emotions of a time when we used to think about and believe in national ideals and universal human aspirations for something pure and sacred.*

. . . The notes that follow are not intended as an exhaustive account of the ins and outs of the Jewish question which riveted the public's attention from October 1940 until several years later and created a great number of difficulties for Bulgaria in its internal affairs. This question damaged our reputation abroad, for it gave others the impression that we enjoyed only limited latitude in the handling of our domestic affairs, insofar as Germany maintained an interest in them as well.

In the years prior to the Second World War, Bulgaria had no 'Jewish question', strictly speaking. Of course we had had a

---

*Peshev intended this text as a foreword to his memoirs.

handful of incidents on the part of small groups that fashioned themselves after the German Nazis and took to the streets in Nazi-style uniforms, spouting borrowed slogans. In striving so hard to imitate the Nazis, these groups neglected to take the country's actual situation into account. We had even had a certain Kunchev, who put on all the airs of a Nazi führer. But all this amounted to little more than a grotesque and pathetic vaudeville that was laughed off the stage and was soon forgotten. Other than that, we had been hearing insistent grumblings from certain sectors and from certain individuals over the role of the Jews in Bulgaria's economic life. The Jews, they said, were becoming more powerful than the Bulgarians and were usurping their places; they were taking control of everything, especially commerce. Soon it was being said that they had managed to infiltrate the industrial sector as well, using their access to credit in order to gain control over various enterprises, initially through stock-market transactions. In the beginning, these rumours rankled with those in the business sector, whose interests were directly implicated; they then spread to wider circles, where the socio-economic aspects of the question were taken up.

In reality, Jews played only a limited role in the commercial credit system, an extensive network of savings banks and credit unions that dispersed loans across vast sectors of the economy. This network, dense and powerful, was managed and controlled by the Central Cooperative Bank, which later merged with the Agrarian Bank, through a series of intermediate mergers with the Central Credit Cooperative and the Union of Cooperative Banks. All of these institutions were led by officers who believed in and were devoted to the cooperatives. These banking institutions had enormous funds at their disposal, in the form of several billion leva in stocks and other investments. Thus most firms and even private individuals had easy access to affordable credit that was liberally extended by publicly established and publicly controlled cooperatives. As for large loans extended to commercial and industrial enterprises, they were dispersed mainly by the Bank for Bulgarian Credit, which had been chartered in 1934, after a series of mergers of several private banks that the economic crisis had brought to the brink of failure. This bank was immediately placed under the control of the People's Bank, whose representative sat in on all meetings of the Bank for Bulgarian Credit's board of directors and had veto power over its decisions; the board itself was made up mostly of representatives of major economic agents from all economic sectors, yet they did not represent financial or stockholders' interests.

Apart from the Bank for Bulgarian Credit, there were other private banks of some importance: the Credit Bank, the Banque Franco-Belge, the Commerce Bank. It was primarily to big businesses that these banks granted loans, in which Jews played a major role, notably at the Banque Franco-Belge. The Credit Bank had been started up by German capital and was directed by a Bulgarian. There was also limited Jewish participation in the area of credit banking, and some Jewish capital there as well. I do not know whether capital that derived from Jewish speculative activities played any role in the private banking system. Perhaps such capital did exist, but how could it have existed alongside this wide network of conventional institutions of every type and scope, from the smallest to the largest? This is a question I cannot answer.

It is true that the Jews had made some inroads into the commercial sector. One could even go so far as to say that they had made great gains not only in the small- and medium-sized business sectors, but in major commercial activities. This was the principal and most visible sphere of their activity. It was this that gave rise to the widespread notion that the Jews played a major role in the economy, a conclusion that ignored the fact that alongside rich and prosperous Jews there were many poor workers and artisans, and that is something else again.

Anti-Jewish attitudes that arose in purely economic sectors, as well as on the battlefield of competition, and, in certain cases, out of personal interest, had found, thanks to the new developments in Germany, a climate receptive to their overt expression and expansion into other spheres.

In other areas of life – spiritual, intellectual, political, social, literary, artistic – Jews had always played a very limited and unimportant role – in some cases they played no role at all. One can safely say that there was not a single Jew in the administration, in the judiciary, or in the army. Nor were there Jewish schoolteachers or university professors in the national education system. Apart from the economic sphere, Jews belonged to the liberal professions. There was a relatively large number of Jewish lawyers, doctors, dentists, pharmacists, and, later, engineers. Jews had no presence whatsoever in the newspaper and magazine industry or, for that matter, any influence over public opinion. In Germany, as we know, the National Socialists had made an issue of the role of the Jews in the press, claiming that a large number of newspapers, some of them important and with a wide circulation, were in Jewish hands. It was also said that the Jews had used these newspapers in an anti-German spirit to influence public opinion, and that a good many university professors and judges were themselves Jews who carried out their duties in a way that was harmful to German interests. In our country, one could not really make such claims; neither in the press, nor in secondary and higher education, nor in the judiciary, was the situation in any way the same.

As to the racial question, Bulgaria did not make an issue of it in the way the National Socialist Party in Germany had. The theory of racial purity had no partisans among Bulgarians, apart from a negligible number of people who had little influence. Among the putative reasons for the Law for the Defence of the Nation, introduced into the National Assembly by the minister of internal affairs on 7 October 1940, was that 'the Bulgarian state and the Bulgarian people have always striven to preserve the integrity of their national character and, most important, have been entirely successful in this regard. The Bulgarian state is wholly national and our nation has maintained its purity to a degree rarely attained in Europe.' Later in the same document, the minister explained that 'This goal may not have made sense in the past; conditions were different then, and people had different ideas. Today, however, the nation has a no less legitimate need to ensure its defence, particularly with regard to international or internationally supported clandestine organizations that might seek to exert an anti-national influence within the Jewish community, which, as part of the international Jewish community, has remained alien to the Bulgarian spirit and represents a danger to the nation state, not only by virtue of its cosmopolitan connections but also in its individual or organized activities of a potentially suspect or anti-national character.' These, then, are the reasons, almost verbatim, advanced in favour of the bill that sought to safeguard the legitimate defence of the nation which, it was maintained, had supposedly managed to preserve its purity.

In our country, mixed marriages between Bulgarians and Jews were very rare and were never considered a threat to the purity of the race, no more so than other mixed marriages, for example, between Bulgarians and Germans, which were relatively more frequent. In the reasons given for the bill, the major emphasis was placed on something else, namely, 'international or internationally supported clandestine organizations that might seek to exert an anti-national influence within the Jewish community, which, as part of the international Jewish community, has remained alien to the Bulgarian spirit and represents a danger to the nation state'.

What the authors of the bill had in mind here was above all the secret Freemason organization which supposedly was promoting anti-national ideas. Never having been a Freemason myself, I had no direct knowledge of the internal workings of this organization. I did know, however, that some members of the Bulgarian social and cultural elites, whom no one would have suspected of playing such an anti-national role, had been or were still members of the Freemasons. I knew that Gabrovski himself, our minister of internal affairs who had drafted and introduced the law, had been a Freemason, as had Professor Filov, the prime minister; the late P. Midilov, our ex-prime minister, had been president of his lodge. It was absurd to think that an organization with such well-placed members would have used its international connections to our country's detriment, especially since, as we know, the Bulgarian Freemasons had in fact used their international connections to defend Bulgaria and advance its interests. It was plain that, in this particular case, the arguments we were now hearing were the same ones used by the German National Socialists who saw the Freemasons as their international rivals. How much real basis did the Germans have for making this argument? I will not take a position on this question because that accusation does not concern us and I do not have good information. But in Bulgaria, this suspicion, which was put forth as one of the reasons in favour of the law, was far from being substantiated; in fact, it was utterly absurd.

The proposed Law for the Defence of the Nation was intended primarily to deal with this question of Freemasonry. The Jews came next. I have already gone briefly over their actual economic role, a subject that had generated interest and caused concern within Bulgarian society. The reasons advanced in favour of the bill did not broach this aspect, but the bill itself contained a number of detailed measures relating to landholdings of persons of Jewish origin (Clause 4) and to the Jews' professional and economic activities (Clause 5). These measures barred Jews from participation in the country's economic life and were later expanded through a series of amendments and appendices as well as through the specific statutes that had to do with its implementation. A special tax and certain other measures compounded the severity of the restrictions, by drastically reducing the political and other rights of the Jews, and, additionally, by requiring them to wear the yellow star so as to set them apart wherever they went, thus limiting their freedom of movement.

In the reasons given for the law, it was said that 'the Jewish community, as part of the international Jewish community, has remained alien to the Bulgarian spirit and represents a danger to the nation state, not only by virtue of its cosmopolitan connections but also in its individual or organized activities of a potentially suspect or anti-national character'. This in fact was the primary objective: to ban any activity that could ultimately affect Bulgaria in some negative way. It should be noted, however, that during the debates on the bill and on its implementation, no facts or concrete evidence were produced to confirm the suppositions or speculations that were offered as grounds for its enactment; these suppositions and speculations were to remain just that – suppositions and vague speculation; the actions and events that would have corroborated them never materialized.

Introduction of the bill into the National Assembly provoked a variety of responses in Bulgarian society. Naturally, the most vehement opposition came from the Jews themselves. The Central Consistory of Jews sent petitions stating that Bulgaria's 46,000 or so Jews constituted an integral and indivisible part of the Bulgarian people and culture, that the

Jews had always coexisted harmoniously with their compatriots, and that during the wars, they had fulfilled their duty as citizens by fighting alongside the Bulgarians and shedding their fair share of blood (950 victims). These petitions recalled that at the Congress of Minorities at the end of the First World War, the Jews had ardently defended the cause of Bulgarian national minorities. They also pointed out that Jews who had left Bulgaria for Palestine were clearly still attached to our country, and that these feelings of attachment had been observed by many Bulgarian travellers to Palestine, some of them famous. The Consistory's petitions also examined in detail the question of Jewish participation in Bulgaria's political life and concluded that this participation was not nearly as important as some imagined. The vast majority of Jews, they maintained, were people of modest means, workers and artisans; one had only to look at their miserable neighbourhoods to get an idea of their poverty. It would be completely wrong, they said, to generalize from the department stores on Léger Street and Târgovska Street and draw conclusions from them about all Jews.

The petitions pointed out other things as well: that the Jews were barred from participating in the ownership of the Bulgarian people's greatest wealth, namely, its land; that they could not be employed in our vast civil service; that they were prevented from taking a leading role in the cultural sphere: the press, literature, music, theatre, art; that, according to the most recent statistics, there were only eighty-four Jewish industrialists and not a single banker, whereas the only Jewish bank – the Guela – with assets of less than 25 million leva, was actually a credit union, and that apart from the Guela, there were only two or three small banks with assets ranging from 250,000 to 2 or 3 million leva; that in Sofia the number of Jews practising the liberal professions amounted to a grand total of 237 – 84 doctors, 58 lawyers, 25 engineers, and 70 dentists –

since Jews were not allowed to hold jobs in the municipal or public service sectors. In these petitions, one could sense that the Jews took their exclusion from military service as a slight to their honour; one could also sense their fear of impoverishment as a direct and indirect result of the restrictions, since a shutdown of Jewish businesses would surely throw labourers and white-collar employees out of work. They also disputed claims of a higher rate of delinquency among Jews, and statistical data were cited proving that the rate of delinquency among the Jewish population was no higher than – and in fact was even lower than – among the rest of the population. In general, the statements of the Consistory refuted the arguments put forward in defence of the proposed law.

The shock that the bill produced was felt across wide sectors of society, and a number of organizations went so far as to send letters containing critical statements that hit their mark. The Lawyers' Union sent a special statement to the prime minister, insisting that the government abandon the bill, which they called 'unnecessary, socially harmful, and contrary to our legal system and to all principles of justice'.* In their cogently argued letter, the lawyers maintained that the restrictive and humiliating measures that were to be imposed on the Jews were not justified by the interests of the state or of the people and ran counter to the democratic spirit of Bulgaria's freedom-loving people, 'who, in all the long years of the Ottoman yoke and its miseries, misfortunes, and injustices, never considered the Jews their enemies or oppressors'. Referring to the statements by the minister of internal affairs himself (that 'the Bulgarian state is wholly national and our nation has maintained its purity to a degree rarely attained in Europe'), the lawyers maintained that the Jewish community constituted no threat to our economy, culture, or national

*See p. 49.

purity. Under these circumstances, they said, there was no national necessity that might require a law that made outcasts of an entire category of Bulgarian citizens and morally degraded them.

The letter also commented on the unfortunate lot of Bulgarian national minorities living abroad under foreign rule and spoke of the pain and outrage that their plight aroused among Bulgarians at home. Our concern and our struggles to defend these oppressed minorities, the lawyers wrote, would lose much of their legitimacy and their moral foundations if we imposed restrictions and arbitrary measures on one of our own minorities. The letter also rejected any restrictions on the professional activities of Jewish lawyers. Lastly, the statement took up the legal aspects of the question, and demonstrated convincingly that the new measures were in contradiction of the Constitution and its provisions concerning the equality of citizens before the law, given that the Jews' political and civil rights were being violated.

It also emerged that a diverse group of Bulgarian writers had sent a letter to the prime minister, demanding that 'in the name of civilization and so as to preserve Bulgaria's good name', he 'stop the enactment of this law whose dire consequences will bring dishonour to our legislature and leave the saddest of memories'.*

The writers who had signed the letter shared their puzzlement that such a law had been thought necessary in Bulgaria, which was not being attacked or threatened by anyone whatsoever. They also expressed their conviction that such a law would be damaging to the Bulgarian people and would leave a black page in our modern annals. The letter went on to point out that throughout our long history, Bulgarians had faced persecution and humiliation; should we then embark on

*See p. 46.

a dangerous path and renounce our status as a free and civilized people? Our goal, they said, was to uphold the country's reputation in the eyes of the civilized world and to warn responsible parties that they, the writers, would not accept the passage of a bill that would tarnish our country's reputation and soil our hard-won traditions of religious tolerance and humanism. This was the gist of the letter from a group of writers, including T. Vlaikov, Elin-Pelin, S. Chilingirov, G. Cheshmedjiev, T. Kunev, E. Bagryana, and Liliev, among others.

The Physicians' Union also took a position against the bill, contesting its restrictions as well as the need for it. Grave consequences were predicted should it be passed. I do not have in hand the exact text of the statement and thus cannot discuss it in detail.

It was also learned that Dimo Kazasov had sent a letter to the prime minister, violently objecting to the premises and intent of the law in every aspect and warning of dire consequences, both at home and abroad.*

For the most part, these letters made no mention of the external pressure that had motivated the law in the first place; they were also silent on the fact that the measures against the Jews were somehow connected with our foreign policy. The sole exception is the allusion to 'imitation' in the writers' declaration. Nevertheless, it was commonly understood that the anti-Jewish measures were being taken for foreign policy reasons and in concurrence with German policy – which explained both the importance that the bill gave to the Jewish question and the severity of the measures against the Jewish community, measures which were supposedly made necessary by this community's activities against German policy and the German people, both inside Germany itself and abroad. We in

*See p. 58.

Bulgaria had heard these accusations before and were well aware of the harsh measures that the German authorities were taking against the Jews in the occupied countries, but we had no idea of the scale of the persecutions in the concentration camps or what was taking place in them; we did not find out about all this until after the war.*

At this time, however, the role of the Jewish question in our foreign policy and its importance in our relations with Germany were not brought up. Nor did these questions come up during the parliamentary debates on the bill. The issue was presented as a purely domestic affair and its resolution was sought on domestic grounds. In time, particularly after the war, it became apparent of course that this had not been entirely the case. I should say, however, that even when the question first came up, I was of the firm conviction that all this was indeed about bringing Bulgarian policies in line with those of Germany, since the Germans attached great importance to the Jewish question and blamed the international Jewish community for the negative attitude of the entire world towards the Germans and their policies. As things stood, it was up to Bulgarian society to draw its own conclusions: some felt that our policies towards Germany – which it was hoped would result in Bulgaria's attaining its principal objectives – justified the anti-Jewish measures, since these policies served Germany's interests.[†] That being said, no one imagined that the measures would become permanent, let alone that they would take the same forms and proportions as those that were being carried out in Germany, which we would only hear of after the war.

The bill, however, did have its supporters. First among

*Note, however, that Peshev's protest letter of March 1943 already speaks of mass murder.

†Bulgaria expected Germany to restore Thrace and Macedonia to Bulgarian rule.

them were the economic milieus, who denounced the role of the Jews in the country's economic life. The Jews, they claimed in their letters, dominated the economy, and this, they said, posed a clear and present danger to the country. The Bulgarian Merchants' Union did not take an official stand, but delegated the responsibility for resolving this 'matter of state' to the government. Declarations also came from various groups of 'economic agents representing unions of merchants, industrialists, and artisans', which pointed to specific instances of Jewish involvement in business, citing, for example, the Berov and Horinsk textile works, supposedly taken over by Jews, and the Banque Franco-Belge, also alleged to have been taken over by Jews through some shady transactions. These charges of course could not be substantiated. To cite one instance, the letter from the 'economic agents representing unions of merchants, industrialists, and artisans' explained the methods used by Jews and Jewish firms to take over and run Bulgarian firms: supposedly, they would seduce Bulgarians and then use them to do the bidding of their Jewish masters. For the most part, charges that the Jews constituted a danger to the country centred on their role in the economic sector. Thus while approving of the law in principle, these usually anonymous statements at the same time maintained that these measures, which were necessary to prevent economic harm to the country, had been deliberately stalled. They alleged, moreover, that the measures did not go far enough or were too weak, and they called for harsher ones. To this end, they proposed concrete revisions of this or that paragraph in the draft bill. One of the suggestions was that Jewish participation in the country's economy be reduced to a level proportionate to the percentage of Jews in the total population.

There were also quite a few debates on the matter of who should qualify as a Jew. The question of the few Jewish converts to Christianity also came up, triggering one particular debate over whether Jewish origins counted under all circumstances. This question drew the Church into the controversy and caused considerable problems for the government.

Support for the law came from other organizations as well and created a great stir. The Bulgarian Students' Union issued a proclamation endorsing the law which, it was claimed, was relatively lenient on the Jews; it called for immediate steps to be taken to put an end to Jewish interference in Bulgaria's economy. According to this student organization, Bulgaria was 'the only country to have unconditionally accepted the domination of Jewish international capital, which in its greed has not only strangled numerous Bulgarian businesses but now is trying to play a role in our nation's cultural and economic life, a role whose anti-national tendencies were all too obvious'. The declaration vehemently denounced responses against the bill from the lawyers' and doctors' unions, as well as the letter from the writers' union. It implied that these positions merely betrayed the influence of the same powerful forces (Jewish economic interests) and that it was high time that Bulgaria put an end to this sad state of affairs.

For the authors of this declaration, the fact that there were Bulgarians who accepted and even defended this intolerable situation of Jewish domination was morally inadmissible; they considered 'the official pretext of defending the Constitution' to be no more than a clumsy attempt to obfuscate certain ulterior motives. These motives, they said, 'are those of men who have lost all sense of responsibility and who hold formal legitimacy and vague notions of humanitarianism above the nation's interests'. The declaration went on to say that 'When important national questions are at stake, neither the lawyers' union, nor the doctors' union, nor the writers who have put their names to a brilliant defence of the Jews have said a single word in defence of Bulgarian national rights. All it took was a handful of mild restrictions on Jews for them to jump to the defence of an intolerable situation that has nevertheless been tolerated until now. But their actions ill serve the cause they want to defend, because they prove once again just how craftily set is the snare with which they intend to strangle any effort on the part of the Bulgarian people to defend themselves.' The students closed their statement by blaming all Bulgarians who, in their negligence, had tolerated Jewish economic domination in Bulgaria. The statement ended with these words: 'Bulgaria's youth is on the alert and will hold to account all those who, at the present hour, are choosing to defend international Jewry rather than fight for Bulgarian national ideals.'

The Bulgarian Youth League came out with its own statement. The League declared itself the enemy of the Jewish contingent which, as a foreign element, 'profits economically from the Bulgarian element at whose expense it thrives. Local Jewry,' it claimed, 'takes advantage of the freedoms granted it by an obsolete constitution in order to advance the cause of international Jewry.' It also spoke of 'this unfortunate characteristic of the Bulgarians, their so-called tolerance', that is used by all the foreign elements, above all the Jews, to serve their own ends. This 'unfortunate characteristic' was to blame for there being only 7 million Bulgarians rather than many more, and also for the Jewish community's having managed to infiltrate our economy to its very depths and occupy the highest positions in our economic hierarchy. In hiding behind Bulgarian names that they have acquired in the officers' reserves, this statement claimed, and by taking advantage of the political naivety of many of our public figures, the Jews supposedly had been able to conquer Bulgaria economically. This statement cited a handful of financial figures concerning income, profits, and capital holdings. The average annual income among the Bulgarian urban population was 1067 leva per capita, whereas Jews from the same population sector were said to earn as much as 26,110 leva per capita. Bulgarian merchants made an annual per capita profit of 371 leva; Jewish merchants earned 10,819. The Jews, it was claimed, controlled 80 per cent of the country's wholesale commerce, and, in certain industries, as much as 85 per cent.

Given the relatively small number of Jews in Bulgaria, these figures looked especially damning: there was one Jew for every hundred Bulgarians, yet a single Jew, by this account, was making profits equal to that of thirty people. These facts, the declaration concluded, demonstrated that Bulgarians were not the most tolerant people in the world so much as the stupidest. The cited data appeared doubtful on the face of it and the speculations accompanying them were far from persuasive. As to the Law for the Defence of the Nation, the declaration claimed that, as a measure intended to put a halt to Jewish exploitation, it had a long way to go; for this reason, the restrictions against the Jews as called for by the law would be useless and vain. They were half-measures at best, and the law might just as well be called the Law for the Defence of the Jewish Nation. In a later section, the declaration brutally attacked the letters from the lawyers, doctors, and writers, and said that all Bulgarians were disgusted by these letters. These lawyers, doctors, and writers were the perfect 'picture of an intelligentsia that had lost its spiritual bearings and had embarked on the path to easy profit and treason'. The Youth League's statement said that the lawyers and doctors lacked the most basic feelings of national loyalty, since their treasonous activities constituted a direct attack on the interests of the Bulgarian people. Towards the end of the declaration, it was claimed that the writers, doctors, and lawyers could not be so naive as to pin their hopes and ideals on notions of order and legality, when the byword of this new day was Justice. The statement ended on a pathetic note: 'The Bulgarian people know what their intelligentsia is up to: its path of advancement is paved with the corpses of its enemies, declared or unknown, who dared stand in the way of its steady and unbridled growth.'

Another group that defended the law was the semi-official Brannik youth group. This organization had included the Jewish question in its political programme and had participated openly in anti-Jewish activities. According to its programme, the Jews were parasites and plunderers. The Brannik maintained that the Jews used their economic control of the economy to dominate every aspect of Bulgarian culture, that they were a conduit for 'modernism', an idea that had sapped the foundations of Bulgarian culture and permeated large sectors of the working class, and that all of this was the result of the Jewish ties to foreign interests. That is why, far from being a strictly economic problem in our country, the Jewish question attacked the specificity of Bulgarian culture. Moreover, the Brannik claimed, in our country the Jewish question was also a racial question, deeply connected with that of the supposed purity of our blood. According to this organization, mixed marriages were on the rise. The increase was attributed to the systematic efforts of the headquarters of international Jewry to reinvigorate the degenerate Jewish race with Bulgarian blood, to establish social and political alliances, and, above all, to strangle our country's anti-Jewish movement while it was still in an embryonic stage. The Brannik youth programme berated Bulgarian men and women, who for the sake of 'money and comfort' had sold their social position and their most precious possession, namely, Bulgarian blood. Bulgaria, they contended, was not alone in its struggle against the Jewish 'scourge'; this battle defined the 'New Europe', and the Brannik were mobilizing their forces and preparing to bring the struggle against this dangerous enemy to its successful conclusion.

In the Assembly debates, the bill encountered vehement

criticism from the opposition, which is not to suggest that the government majority was unanimous in its support for the law. A good many deputies objected to the law both in principle and as a practical matter. And yet the split within the majority on this question did not become public and was never a source of open conflict, because the adversaries agreed that the pressing political issues of the day took precedence; in the interest of overall national policy and the needs of the state itself, the dissenters resigned themselves to the sacrifice required of them. This sacrifice was made more palatable by the knowledge that the restrictions on the Jews, however painful, were nonetheless temporary and would not be taken to extremes. Thus the law was passed in a somewhat amended form; it was promulgated and took effect in January 1941. Later, the regulations governing its implementation would be published and official bodies created to see that these regulations were carried out. The selection of members of the Commissariat, as the central executive body in charge of applying the law was called, was an unfortunate one. The Commissariat would be headed by a person notorious for his extreme anti-Jewish attitudes.* This person allowed his personal convictions to interfere with his duties, and many of his decisions betrayed malice. None of this favoured the creation of a climate in which the many difficulties and enormous frustrations of applying an extremist law could have been avoided.

I am not familiar with the details of the law's implementation, or with its material, financial, personal, logistical, and other aspects. We would hear the occasional report about certain Jews who were having trouble subsisting, as well as complaints about the Commissariat, its practices and relations, which resulted from the prevailing atmosphere within the

*Alexander Belev.

organization. A heavy tax had been imposed on the Jews and steps had been taken to ensure compliance with the law's provisions concerning the professional and private property of persons of Jewish origin. These harsh measures triggered a number of debates, mostly on the question of how to determine the status of certain persons in view of the various and sometimes conflicting interpretations of a number of different legal texts on the question of Jewish identity. Some held that the proper thing to do was to recognize the Jewish origins of socially prominent individuals and hold these individuals to the law and its provisions, for example, the requirement to wear the yellow star. This sort of observation baffled some of the deputies, and it became clear that a decision had to be made if absurd excesses were to be avoided. For the most part, the deputies were not at all inclined to approve these extreme positions and instead preferred a narrower definition of 'Jewish origins'. Ultimately, the narrower definition prevailed, and a number of public figures whose meritorious service to the country was well known were spared the effects of a harsher implementation of the law, this notwithstanding the objections of a few deputies who had diametrically opposite opinions as to how the matter should have been resolved.

And so implementation of the measures continued, sometimes in fits and starts and not without pain, yet somehow the worst extremes were avoided. The situation seemed to hold out hope that the question might be resolved without further complications or recourse to new measures. This new hope was reinforced by a statement from Minister of Internal Affairs Gabrovski, who at the majority caucus of 19 September 1942, in which the government's domestic policies were under discussion, had declared that it was time to begin putting the Jewish question behind us. The whole issue had taken on unwarranted proportions and we needed to apply the law in a 'reasonable, humane, and moral way'. Those of us who, in a climate rife with rumour and apprehension, had come to fear additional and more stringent anti-Jewish measures, took comfort in this news.

I was not privy to the developments that took place within government circles during the winter of 1942–3. Only after the war did some bits and pieces of information finally reach me. Dramatic events were unfolding during those days, which could have had tragic consequences for the Jews, or at least for some of them, undoubtedly damaging Bulgaria's reputation for ever. Moreover, these events could have had dire political consequences for our country and undermined the moral bulwarks of its national policy. What exactly happened in the inner recesses of the government policy apparatus? I am not able to say, and that is why I can shed only dim light on this question, perhaps to the disappointment of all those who might have expected more of me. My involvement in these dramatic events was purely parliamentary, and, paradoxically, it may have been precisely this restricted scope of my involvement that lent force and importance to my activities. Future historians will no doubt have access to all the relevant sources and documents, and perhaps to eyewitness accounts by some of those who participated in the events of the time, should any such accounts remain, as well as to information from Bulgarian and foreign diplomatic archives; future scholars, then, should be able to study the events with a critical objectivity, without being influenced either by propaganda considerations or by political or personal interests of any kind. By acting fairly and in the name of historical truth, they will be able to determine the exact sequence of events and the role played by the various factors in the resolution of this problem.

And now, as objectively as I can, I shall set down the events that took place at the National Assembly – or, I should say, what I remember of them, for I took no notes at the time –

along with my own role in them. I will comment only on what I know for certain to be true and will point out where I am not absolutely certain of my recollections. I have no desire whatsoever to turn my recollections into a self-serving exercise, for I am convinced that the objective historical truth would be sacrificed in any attempt to make it serve personal ends.

The present account, then, deals with what happened in the National Assembly, which was only one of the sites where the dramatic events related to the Jewish question occurred. If, after further research, future historians come to the conclusion that this arena played a decisive role that also proved useful to the country, I would feel a great sense of moral satisfaction, since it was there that my interventions took place. For now, I will refrain from drawing such conclusions, because I am presenting only a part of what transpired. Let my readers draw their own independent conclusions from the facts that I will scrupulously and objectively set forth.

I was expectantly awaiting a solution to this difficult Jewish question which, to use the words of the minister of internal affairs himself, needed to be resolved in a 'reasonable, humane, and moral way', when rumours of troubles in the new territories began to reach us. In Thrace and Macedonia, new measures had reportedly been taken against the Jews. We had had no official confirmation of this news, and no explanation was forthcoming as to the nature of these measures or whether they were confined to these regions. I attributed these developments to the fact that Germany had greater authority in these territories, which had not been officially annexed to Bulgaria. This was only a hypothesis; in fact there were no differences between these territories and other regions of Bulgaria in terms of their administration. I heard that what these new measures entailed was nothing more and nothing less than the mass round-up of men, women, and children, who were then taken away somewhere – but we did not know where. What was the nature of these measures? Where were all the Jews, regardless of age or sex, being sent? And for what reason? Everything was shrouded in mystery; the possible explanations were limitless; meanwhile dramatic, even tragic, images kept coming to mind.

As I was trying to understand what was happening and why, I received a visit from Dimitâr Ikonomov, the deputy to the National Assembly from the town of Dupnitsa. He and I had had our differences on certain issues that had come up in the Assembly, and our relations had grown so strained that we were no longer on speaking terms. I was therefore surprised to see him. I believed him to be a decent man and an upstanding public servant who was deeply committed to the interests of his home town and the electoral college of Dupnitsa. He told me that he had just returned from a visit there and was extremely depressed by what he had witnessed taking place in the street. He described a distressing scene – Thracian Jews, old people, men, women, and children, carrying their belongings, defeated, desperate, powerless people, begging for help as they crossed the town on foot, dragging themselves towards some unknown destination. He was saddened and utterly outraged to see helpless people being sent to some destination that could only be surmised, to a fate that conjured up everyone's darkest fears. He spoke of the effect of this horrible scene on the residents of Dupnitsa, their anger and outrage, their inability to remain indifferent to the tragedy that was unfolding before their eyes: this multitude of women and children and old people who were being taken who knows where. To hear Ikonomov tell it, the townspeople's despair was so great that many had been moved to tears.

This detailed description by an eyewitness upset me as well: the rumours I had been hearing were true. I do not recall the exact date of my meeting with Ikonomov, but it must have been in early March 1943. Shortly thereafter, I went to Kyustendil, where the assistant chief of police informed me that preparations were under way to assemble all local Jews in a single location – some empty tobacco warehouses. They had been instructed to bring along their personal effects. This same man also informed me that an order had been issued to provide them with buckets for water as well as sanitary buckets for nature's needs. From then on, things were clear. It was obvious where all these preparations were leading. For all the trouble that had been taken to keep things quiet, the secret could no longer be hidden, especially since we had heard that a representative from the Commissariat for Jewish Questions had arrived in town. His mission was to begin implementing a decision concerning the Jews. I returned to Sofia but remained in contact with the assistant chief of police who had informed me of the order to round up the Jews and hold them in the empty warehouses. The operation was to take place at night, special convoys were already starting to form or were expected to arrive shortly, and their departure times had already been set. There could be no more doubt about what was going to happen to the Jews.

I then recalled the tragic scene that Dimitâr Ikonomov had described to me. I could not remain passive – my conscience and understanding of the grave consequences both for the people involved and for my country did not allow it. It was then that I made the decision to do everything in my power to prevent the execution of a plan that was going to compromise Bulgaria in the eyes of the world and brand it with a mark of shame that it did not deserve. I would not assume any moral, political, or any other responsibility for actions that the government had decided to take without consulting the National Assembly or receiving its approval. Up until that time, the anti-Jewish measures had been explicitly or tacitly sanctioned by the Assembly, which had passed the Law for the

Defence of the Nation. The measures that the majority had approved, in spite of their severity, in the name of the higher interest of the nation and the state, did not include the extermination of the Jews. But that was exactly where we were heading if the operation that was now being prepared, and that needed only to be set in motion, was not halted: Jews would be deported and consigned to a fate of which we had only a vague notion but were now beginning to fathom.

It was just then that the residents of Kyustendil sent a delegation to Sofia to intercede on behalf of Bulgarian Jews to prevent their deportation. I informed the delegation – I. Momchilov, a lawyer; A. Suichmezov, a merchant; and V. Kurtev – of the steps that I, together with other deputies, were planning to take and I told them that in presenting my case I intended to mention them and their fellow citizens who had sent them here. I also told them that their personal intervention and their presence here or anywhere else for that matter was not absolutely necessary; in short, that I and my friends were going to do everything we could.

The first thing I needed to do was to go at once to see the minister of internal affairs, whose responsibilities included dealing with the Jewish question, and gather what information I could from him about the recent events. I would also let him know, in the strongest possible terms, that we could neither accept nor approve nor shoulder the responsibility for the new measures being taken against the Jews, and that we intended to fight them regardless of the consequences. At the National Assembly, rumours of impending new measures against the Jews were already circulating. These rumours may have surfaced following my telephone conversation with the assistant chief of police of Kyustendil who, in spite of his orders to secrecy, had told me of the instructions stipulating the round-up of Jews during the night, their detention in designated tobacco warehouses, the departure times of the special convoys now waiting at the station, ready to transport them to an undisclosed destination – and had let me know of the arrival in Kyustendil of the special agent from the Commissariat for Jewish Questions who was to oversee the execution of these orders. It is also possible that this information had been communicated to other provincial deputies by sources in other towns where similar preparations were under way. Whatever the source of the news, the deputies were deeply troubled by it, and some of them approached me for further information and to find out how we were going to proceed. Several deputies supported my proposal that we begin by going to see the minister, and it was decided that a group of us would meet him to apprise him of the deputies' position and the extent of the reaction against the measures. I do not remember what day of the week this was, and consequently I cannot be sure of the exact date of these developments, but it was around 10 March 1943.*

The minister of internal affairs was at the National Assembly that day and the regular session was about to begin. I do not remember the precise composition of our group, but I am certain it included Petâr Mikhalev, Dimitâr Ikonomov, and Tsvyatko Petkov. There were ten of us in all. The minister received us immediately. I briefed him on the information I had received. I also informed him of our fears, our disapproval of the measures, our refusal to take responsibility for them, and our urgent request that they be cancelled. The minister said that we had nothing to worry about, that no new anti-Jewish measures existed, and he promised to find out what exactly was happening. I, for one, was impressed by how tense and nervous he seemed, and although his assurance that there were no new measures specifically targeting the Jews was hard to believe, since it completely contradicted what I knew to be

---

*In fact, it was 9 March 1943.

unimpeachable information, I really did not suspect that he was trying to trick us with outright lies. It occurred to me that he was speaking in the kind of platitudes one might use to extricate oneself from an awkward situation, and at any rate, it looked as though the plans for deportation were going to be abandoned. This satisfied and reassured me for the moment, since our primary concern had been to prevent the deportations.

The following day brought news that the preventive measures calling for the Jews to be assembled all in one place in view of transporting them somewhere had been suspended. The other news that day was that measures similar to those that had been taken in Kyustendil had also been taken in other towns, where local Jews, regardless of sex and age, had been rounded up during the night, assembled in one place, and put on the trains. In some cases, they were already on board when the order was lifted. The cancellation of these measures brought hope to the Jews and a sense of relief to almost all of their fellow citizens, who opposed these cruel measures that weighed so heavily on their consciences.

But for me and some of my fellow deputies, this relief was temporary; we had been given a moment of reprieve in which to consider what was going to happen next, for we now learned that the Commissar for Jewish Questions and some unnamed representative of the German government had concluded an agreement* bearing on the deportation of 20,000 Bulgarian Jews. We never found out the exact content of that shameful agreement; nor were we able to learn what or who had authorized its signing by a Bulgarian functionary. We could not understand how the fate of thousands of Bulgarian citizens could be decided in a manner that was so contrary to the Constitution as well as to the most basic humanitarian

---

*This was the Dannecker–Belev agreement.

principles. A hard blow had been dealt to Bulgaria's honour, to its international prestige, and to the moral force of its foreign policy, which we had often invoked in the past and were certainly going to have to invoke in the future.

Official confirmation of the existence of this agreement never materialized. Nor were any explanations forthcoming as to why the measures were never carried out, and no one was willing or able to tell us what was to happen next. Everything was shrouded in impenetrable mystery, and we began to suspect that the measures had been lifted only temporarily, especially since the agreement between the Commissar for Jewish Questions and the still unidentified German official was being described as an 'international' one. That agreement, entered into by an incompetent bureaucrat in violation of the Constitution, the ordinary rule of law, common decency and basic human sympathy, could not be implemented and, from a legal standpoint, was null and void. The agreement was thus entirely arbitrary and not an international contract in any legal sense.

I considered what I had to do. I could not fold my arms and sit back quietly when at stake were matters that would have such grave consequences both now and in the future. To remain silent would have been a breach of conscience, it would have been contrary to my sense of responsibility both as a deputy and as a human being. I would be responsible for the outcome if I did not take steps to halt actions that had already begun but were now temporarily suspended and that I knew to be a grave crime from a constitutional as well as a human and moral viewpoint.

I decided to act. But how? A solitary act, though possible, seemed to me both inadequate and ineffectual; it could easily be brushed off and dismissed by the government, which would have undoubtedly claimed that its decisions were justified by the nation's higher interests which, for reasons of state, could not be divulged. I also realized that there was no time to lose, because one could only assume that even though the measures had been suspended, their enforcement could resume at any time, given the likelihood of pressure from the Germans who were obviously interested in this question and would never have accepted the total dissolution of an arrangement that they believed had already been settled.

To achieve the main objective, which was to prevent irreparable harm, I believed it was necessary to bring the question to the Assembly and draw on as large a base as possible within the government majority. The action had to be of a parliamentary nature, it seemed to me, if the government was to get a sense that it was facing a difficult situation in the Assembly, that its majority hung in the balance, and that it had to take this new situation into account. The government was in no position not to do so: it did not have sufficient support among the people, the state apparatus was not secure enough for the government to rule by fiat, and the head of state had little to gain by putting his authority to the test on a question that, by all appearances, remained unpopular. If the government continued on the path it had embarked on and stood by the new anti-Jewish measures, it might well find itself isolated, especially since the measures had been roundly rejected by the Bulgarian intelligentsia. I felt that the initiative had to come from the government majority and that the objective needed to be perfectly targeted; in other words, it had to be made clear that stopping the deportation of Bulgarian Jews once and for all was paramount. Inaction by the majority on this question would have made it an accomplice not only to a crime of state, a violation of the Constitution, but to much more – to criminal felony plain and simple: the mass murder of thousands of human beings. The polity must not be soiled in this way.

On the other hand, it was important not to give the

impression of trying to make matters worse by provoking a
political crisis or by destabilizing the domestic political
situation or Bulgaria's foreign policy. It was crucial that the
action not be construed as an attempt to create a crisis within
the government in order to satisfy the ministerial ambitions of
some individuals. This patently disingenuous argument had
often been used in the past to deflect serious and well-
intentioned criticisms of government measures. Such an
impression had to be avoided if this action, which had been
undertaken with the sole aim of swiftly and safely accomplish-
ing a noble goal, was not to be discredited by attacks on its
moral and political underpinnings.

In short, I was convinced that for the action to succeed, it
had to be led by members of the majority who repudiated
neither the regime nor the general principles of its domestic
and foreign policy nor its own overall support for the
government, but rather disagreed with it on a single issue: the
deportation of Bulgarian Jews and their delivery to a foreign
power whose intentions in their regard no one could claim not
to know. I was convinced that only an action of this type could
find a favourable reception within the Assembly majority, and
I was certain that it would be approved by a significant number
of deputies who shared this aim. To have sought support
beyond the government majority, on the other hand, would
have provoked a political crisis and disrupted Bulgaria's larger,
and moreover fairly promising, national policy; it would also
have cost us the support of a number of individuals in the
majority who, in this case, might have felt that they would
have to take the blame for the failure of major national and
state objectives. It was for this reason that I did not respond to
opposition deputy Petko Stainov, who had told me that he
would sign the declaration if I thought his doing so would be
of some use.

The majority's watchword at the time was the following: we

stand united behind the state's overall policies, which we, as the people's trusted representatives, agree to support because it is the only way to succeed. Accordingly, we had to prevent any intrusion of elements that did not support the government's primary policy goals and that, instead of contributing to their success, could have caused the government irreparable damage. On the other hand, parliamentary action itself, within these constraints, could enhance the Assembly's role and importance, and it was not out of the question that, at some future time, the Assembly could become a valuable element in our country's political life if it now defended Bulgaria's honour and prestige without disrupting the normal course of the state's politics. This position would find support among the majority, whereas the other sort of intervention, with a wider base, a larger scope and broader aims, would certainly not have been well received and would not have won support among the deputies; moreover, the government could easily have discredited it on moral grounds. Our unifying force could only be the desire to prevent Bulgarian citizens from being delivered to a foreign government; we could not make this a question of confidence in the government, especially since the government had never acknowledged its role in the first deportations or taken responsibility for its part in the latest measures. We could thus make the case that our action did not target the government itself; this ought to have reassured those who hesitated to challenge the government directly.

Having thought these questions through, I wrote a letter of protest to the prime minister.*

I signed the letter myself and then turned it over to the other deputies of the majority so that it could be signed in the Assembly by those who agreed with and would endorse its contents. Given that this took place in the afternoon, before

*See p. 78.

the opening of the regular session, all the deputies immediately knew what was happening and a great commotion ensued. Different deputies had different thoughts about what the document meant; some even said it was first-rate; and quite a few deputies wanted to sign it. I stressed the fact that the action was a majority action only, and I accepted the signatures of just two deputies who did not belong to the majority – Alexander Tsankov and Todor Kojukharov. Since they were strong supporters of the government's policies towards Germany, their signatures would make it difficult for our parliamentary action to be constructed as anti-German.*

Many deputies, I noticed, seemed to be relieved to sign it; one could sense the degree to which they had been troubled, the great dismay they had felt in the face of recent events, and the profound awareness they had of their responsibilities. I remember a remark made by the deputy from Breznik, A. Simov, immediately after affixing his signature. 'Bulgaria's honour is safe,' he said. His words captured the feelings and the convictions of many in that company who disapproved of a situation that they had not foreseen and that had taken them by surprise.

In the midst of what now had every sign of being a successful action, I had to inform the chairman of the National Assembly, Christo Kalfov, of our initiative. This, I thought, was the right and loyal thing to do; I did not want our action to be taken as a conspiracy, hatched behind the back of the majority leader. I picked up an unsigned copy of the letter and made my way to his office. I apprised him of the initiative and explained the motives for it. He read the letter without raising a single objection or even commenting on it. After leaving his office, and even before I had taken more than a few steps away, I saw him leave, letter in hand, and proceed towards the wing where the prime minister's office was located. I returned to my

*Both deputies belonged to the right-wing and pro-German opposition.

own office and walked in on several deputies who were busy discussing the events of the afternoon. The scene inside reflected the general excitement in the National Assembly that day. A short time later, the chairman summoned me to his office. I went immediately. He told me that he had transmitted my letter to the prime minister, who had asked him to intercede on his behalf and request that I not submit it at this time but wait until the next majority caucus, where all these questions were to be presented in written form.

I said nothing and left the office to reflect on the meaning of this request by the prime minister and consider what the consequences might be were I not to comply with it. But in any case, I did not interrupt the campaign for signatures; the statement had already been signed by a good number of deputies and might still be signed by others. I had initially anticipated needing two days to gather the signatures of all those who might want to sign. But now, I wondered what hidden motives lay behind the prime minister's request that we postpone sending the letter. Was he attempting to foil our action by trying to gain time in which to exert pressure on the deputies who had already signed it, as well as on those who intended to sign it, and possibly even on those who supported it but had chosen not to sign it? I did not rule out the possibility of institutional pressure, some of it against me; no doubt the government wanted to avoid the publicity surrounding this action whose consequences were as undesirable for the government as they were useful to the aims of the protest. It was obvious that the government was enormously irritated and annoyed, because, in the midst of all this commotion, Minister of Internal Affairs Gabrovski, who it was said had been confined to his bed, telephoned me himself and demanded that I send him a copy of the letter immediately, which I did.

Convinced of the necessity of seeing our intervention through and certain of its usefulness to the attainment of our goal, I decided to ignore the prime minister's request and submit the letter with its forty-two signatures first thing next morning, even if this meant forgoing the others. My haste would no doubt displease some of the deputies, who would be angry that I had deprived them of the opportunity to sign it. Indeed, we could have gathered several more signatures had this sudden urgency not forced my hand. The following morning, I sent the letter to the prime minister and the minister of foreign affairs. I would later learn how irritated he was both by its contents and by my refusal to heed his advice. In the days that followed, he gave vent to his irritation and finally exploded in a fit of anger that expressed both frustration and a desire for revenge.

Several days passed during which I had no idea of what was happening behind closed doors, since no news filtered to the outside. Word had it that the cabinet had taken the question under discussion, and that the prime minister had let it be known in so many words that he intended to take severe measures against nearly all the majority deputies. On 23 March, a majority caucus was convened; every member of the cabinet attended, as did nearly all the deputies belonging to the majority. The atmosphere was heavy from the very beginning, and from the prime minister's sombre demeanour one could see that the meeting would be difficult and unpleasant; one can only regret that no minutes from this meeting have survived. The deputies from the majority were not organized and so it was the prime minister who, acting on behalf of the government, would convene the caucuses, when he judged them necessary and timely. Ordinarily, they were presided over by a deputy to whom the prime minister had delegated this responsibility. This time, however, the meeting was chaired by the prime minister himself, who announced that he had received the protest signed by forty-three deputies and then proceeded to read it aloud in its entirety. He let it be known that I had been advised by him, through the intermediary of the chairman of the National Assembly, not to send the letter until such time as the majority had a chance to convene and debate the matter at hand. He stated that the Assembly chairman had told him that I had agreed to this request, and now, my promise notwithstanding, it seemed that I had gone ahead and sent the letter. All of this was said in scolding and disapproving tones that were difficult to miss. I sat there silently and attentively and heard him out, for it was obvious that all of this – both the content and the tone – was being directed at me. In the interest of historical accuracy, I should make it clear that his assertion that I had promised not to send the letter, but had agreed to wait until the majority had convened, is not factual. I categorically deny ever having made such a promise. Of course, I have no way of knowing how my conversation with the chairman of the Assembly was conveyed to the prime minister, but what I have described here is the truth.

The prime minister's opening remarks left no doubt as to the purpose of this meeting. The position expressed in the petition, he stressed, raised questions of discipline within the majority vis-à-vis the government and had a prejudicial effect on the government's authority; it was absolutely necessary to clarify our relations, so that each side could carry out its responsibilities. In fact, he was accusing us of open rebellion, even though he never said it in so many words. His hectoring tone had its desired effect and several of the deputies were unnerved at the thought of the unpleasant consequences of what we had undertaken. It was obvious that the government did not want to take a position on the contents of the letter or throw open the debate on what it meant. But we could not guess the reasons for this refusal. Throughout the meeting, no mention was made of the concrete questions, that is, the substance and purpose of the letter; it was as though they did not exist. All we heard was reproach and rebuke – how was it possible that certain deputies had broken ranks and taken part in an action that damaged relations with the government? we were asked. Why had they chosen to disregard the government's request not to send the letter before it could be debated in a majority caucus?

In short, the whole affair shifted to a discussion of the deputies' right to present their demands to the ministers and to express their opinions on governmental decisions and on governmental actions that involved the country's higher interests. The responsibility for these actions fell to the deputies as well, insofar as they supported the government and had placed their trust in it. This right, then, was inherent in the duties of the deputy, and I for one was not going to forfeit or compromise that right, at least not without a struggle.

The government apparently saw things differently. Taking advantage of the circumstances, it tried to give the impression that what it wanted was the deputies' approval of the measures it had undertaken. For some reason or other – maybe because most of the deputies were not affiliated with parties or other political organizations that could have supported them, and thus owed their elected positions to the government's good graces; or maybe because they felt that events did not bode well, and hence felt obliged to stand firmly with the government so as to ensure its power and authority at home and abroad – the deputies, at all events, were unwilling to jeopardize their relations with the government or stand in the way of its activities, and they would even go so far as to limit their own rights. Needless to say, such a response is fundamentally wrong, especially when it comes to matters in which mistakes by the government can have serious policy repercussions. If legislators are prepared to take responsibility for governmental policy, they then have the obligation to speak their minds. And that was exactly what we had done in our letter, since it presented reasons that presupposed extremely serious consequences for Bulgaria's present and future policies. Rather than discuss assertions and assessments, as well as the concrete circumstances that had given rise to them, the government insisted on its desire to hold a debate solely on the question of the initiative itself, its nature, how it was carried out, and the attitude of the majority vis-à-vis the government. In this way, the government avoided the issue of the new measures against the Jews and also side-stepped the question of why these measures had been taken and to what hidden ends. It was our action itself, the letter of protest that we had sent to the minister, that was indicted that day; it was declared incompatible with the majority's overall political confidence in the government.

Naturally, I took the floor to respond to the prime minister. I stressed the fact that I had initiated the action, that I had written the protest letter myself, and that I was willing to accept all the blame – insofar as one could speak of blame. For in fact there could be no question of blame, given that everything we had done derived from the incontestable right of every deputy to express his opinions on questions relating to the government and to general policies, to prevent actions that he considered to be ill advised, and to determine the limits of his responsibility to and his confidence in the government. It was not only his right, it was also his duty, and in the case at hand, this duty had been done. One had only to read the text itself – the introduction, the reasons for the open letter – to see that no one had tried to provoke a general political crisis or interfere with the government's general policy, as some had maintained in their disingenuous and tendentious interpretations of our action. Apparently, some people thought that they could easily compromise an action that was pure by definition and that pursued carefully circumscribed political and humanitarian goals that had been explicitly indicated in the letter. The

letter also clearly stated that the deputies who signed it could
not share responsibility for 'exceptional and cruel measures . . .
that may expose the government and the entire nation to
accusations of mass murder', since they had expressed their
conviction that recourse to these measures was totally
unnecessary. I also pointed out that, for me, the letter was not
about the government's general policy, whose implementation, as mentioned in the letter, enjoyed our approval and our
support, but rather about the national policy for the unifica-
tion of the Bulgarian people, in which we were all implicated.

I had just finished these explanations and was feeling
extremely discouraged when the prime minister took the floor
and, in a brutal display of political pressure, asked each man in
turn to answer the following questions: did he approve of the
sending of the letter signed by the forty-three deputies from
the majority, and did he support the government's overall
policies? He was putting the deputies to the test to see
whether those who had signed the letter would now disclaim
it. I later learned that some of the deputies had been
intercepted beforehand and had been asked if they still stood
by their signatures. Some had answered yes, but others had
already withdrawn their signatures. I am not sure who those
others were, so I will not name names – besides it is a useless
question and of no interest whatsoever, especially in the light
of what later came about.* We proceeded to the voting. It
was an excruciating process, an inquisition of sorts, and the
relentless pressure only added to an oppressive atmosphere
that was hardly conducive to the free expression of opinions
and convictions. The deputies were called on one by one, and
each had to stand while answering the questions, as the prime

*Peshev is alluding here to the tragic fate of several of the deputies who
had signed the protest. In 1944, they were sentenced by the People's
Tribunal and executed.

minister, pencil in hand, took notes. Never in my life had I witnessed such a scene. It was a brutal procedure, a cowardly breach of trust, and completely incompatible with the deputies' function. When my turn came, I stood fully behind my letter, as I had already told the caucus, but I also made it entirely clear that I did not reject the government's overall policy, and would continue to give it my full support.

The prime minister must have been pleased by the outcome: only thirty of the forty-three individuals who had signed the letter stood by their signatures and refused to condemn the action, whereas the deputies, to a man, declared their support for the government's overall policies. It was a defeat for me and a victory for the prime minister, who, for reasons that escaped me, said he felt he had been wronged. He gloated in this victory, and did not stop to think about how he had achieved it – with methods that were humiliating for the Assembly, beneath the dignity of his position as prime minister of a constitutional state, and incompatible with the role of the deputies. I cannot say I was calm at this moment, and, as my prerogatives as a deputy had been attacked, I decided to leave. As I stood up to leave the room where many deputies sat, their heads bent, beginning to grasp the full significance of what had just happened and would probably happen again, the prime minister broke the silence and proclaimed in a triumphant voice, '*Tu l'as voulu, Georges Dandin,*' taunting me with this famous and often cited line by the French writer whose name I have forgotten.* The prime minister may have thought himself witty, whereas all he was doing was letting us see the depths of his rancour.

Later, when I had a chance to reflect on what had transpired, what it meant, and the reasons for it, I was struck by the disparity between the force and brutality of the pressure that been exerted against the deputies and the deputies' action

*Molière.

itself, which in both form and content was entirely consistent with parliamentary principles. I was also struck by the calm they had shown throughout the meeting and by the care they took to avoid needless debate and confrontation. The most probable explanation, it seemed to me, was that the prime minister, who must have seen this action as setting a dangerous precedent for future relations between the majority and the government, had actually seized this opportunity to impute intentions to the majority that it did not have. He wanted to do away with the free exercise of parliamentary control, once and for all, and was willing to use violent means to have done with an idea that he found intolerable and could not accept. In this way, he had tried to turn the Assembly majority into an obedient instrument of the government.

And so I left the meeting while it was still in session. I do not know what happened after I left, and even later, I never bothered to find out what had been discussed or decided. The prime minister's attitude, his obvious ill-will, and his sarcastic remarks gave me reason to believe that he was not going to leave it at that but would try to force my removal as vice-chairman of the Assembly. I was disappointed by the lack of conviction, the docility, and the opportunism of some of my colleagues, who had failed to defend their prerogatives as deputies and had yielded under pressure at the expense of parliamentary principles. I was in the grip of these disheartening thoughts, when, quite by chance, I ran into Simon Radev, a famous diplomat, historian, and writer. In fact it was he who stopped me, and he wanted to ask me about rumoured developments surrounding the Jewish question. I gave him a brief account of what had happened in the majority caucus, how the deputies had reacted, and the consequences that all this had for me – namely, the vote of censure that had been brought against me in my capacity as vice-chairman of the National Assembly. He listened attentively, and, as he was taking his leave, he said to me that Bulgaria had committed two errors in her recent past, the first being on 16 June 1913, the day of her attack on her own allies in the Balkan Wars;* the second error, he said, was what she was doing today in the handling of the Jewish question. Those were his words to me before we parted. I was terribly surprised by this comparison, which had never occurred to me. I mention the opinion of this remarkable man and historian so that others who may one day be interested in past and present events might take it into account in drawing their conclusions. I, however, will refrain from doing so.

And so this chapter in the history of the new anti-Jewish measures came to an end, shortly after their implementation had begun. It was still too soon to draw conclusions from this episode, but not too early to make predictions. After all that had happened at the National Assembly and the widespread public disapproval of all the new anti-Jewish measures, particularly those that had called for the deportation of Bulgarian Jews, the government would not broach such measures again. That had been the goal of my letter, and the vote of censure against me and the vindictive attitude of others towards me could not alter the fact that that goal had been achieved. The scene at the National Assembly may have been a smokescreen, designed to hide the fact that the government already had no choice at that time other than to take the steps that my letter advised. It could be that the difficult scene at the caucus and the psychological violence used there were a sign of the government's powerlessness to act otherwise, an expression of wounded pride and thwarted ambitions; otherwise, the government would have had to admit to a mistake, and, in this case, it was a mistake that others had already noted. To do so

*In 1913, during the Second Balkan War, Bulgaria attacked Serbia and Greece, which had been her allies in the First Balkan War. In her defeat, Bulgaria had to give up the provinces of Macedonia, Thrace, and Dobrudja.

would not have been easy for people who had always had
confidence in themselves and until now had never come up
against an obstacle that had forced them to retreat. They no
doubt wanted to disguise their reversal with noisy and
spectacular theatrics in which the deputies, or at least some of
them, would be cast in the role of the guilty or the penitent.
To admit to error on a question of such importance cannot
have been easy for those whose mistake it was; hence their
recourse to the charade at the majority caucus. But psychological violence cannot turn right into wrong. Thus it would be
inaccurate to say that the government had achieved a 'victory'
at the majority caucus when it forced a number of the deputies
to disavow the letter. The fact that even after this vote the
government did not try once more to implement new
measures against the Jews proves that it never benefited from
this 'victory'. Were not this caucus and the procedures used
there intended to deter the deputies from having future
recourse to similar efforts at parliamentary control?

All that remained now was the final act, in which the
consequences of our parliamentary intervention were to play
themselves out. The prime minister, who throughout this
whole story had demonstrated not only spite and violence but
also his anti-democratic ideas about the free exercise of
parliamentary rule, was not going to allow me to remain vice-
chairman of the National Assembly. That was why he tried to
suggest that I resign. It was in this way that the government
intended to resolve the matter and extricate itself from the
predicament in which it found itself, particularly after news of
the inglorious proceedings reached the public who, for the
most part, did not share his views on this question. The
minister of justice, Dr K. Partov, was given the job of
convincing me to submit my resignation. He came to see me
at home, where he tried to persuade me that I should resign
voluntarily in order to spare myself future difficulties and help

lay minds to rest by putting an end to an unpleasant incident. Though he did not admit it openly, I was convinced that Partov, with whom I was on close and friendly terms, did not, in his heart of hearts, approve of the government's behaviour. We knew each other well; we had worked together for many years; I held him in high regard, and it was undoubtedly for these reasons that he had been selected for the mission. Yet despite my affection for the man, I told him categorically that I could not agree to his proposal. We met several times subsequently, always at his initiative and always at my home, and each time my answer was the same.

The more I thought about it, the more I was convinced I could not end the action in this way; it had been a serious step, taken out of a deep conviction that it was the only way to prevent a mistake – a mistake that would have equally serious consequences for the country, its policy, and its honour; that would entail a grave infringement of the Constitution; and, finally, that would have proved fatal to thousands of people. It was my firm belief that I had done my duty as a deputy and had acted in the name of my country's interests and its reputation, and for the sake of humanity; and now I was being asked to do something that would have amounted to capitulation, admission of error, humiliation through self-criticism. In the light of everything that had happened, my resignation would have served to justify the psychological violence exerted against certain deputies who, acting according to their conscience, had defended the principle of parliamentary rule; it would also have demeaned the Assembly and made it easier in the future for the government to keep the legislative body in line. Furthermore, my resignation would have provided the government with an easy way out of the predicament in which its unpardonable behaviour had landed it. And finally, as an act of self-criticism and remorse (which is how my resignation would have been interpreted), it would have signified a repudiation of the moral value of parliamentary action and cast a pall over everything I had done. Those are the reasons for my categorical and final refusal of the proposal that had been made to me. I told Minister Partov that, given the votes that it had at its command in the Assembly, the government should have no trouble obtaining its vote of censure against me. This vote of censure was the only resolution I was willing to accept. Any other, I felt, would have compromised me in the eyes of the Bulgarian people, and instead of coming across as a man of conviction who was fighting for higher objectives and principles, I would have appeared as nothing more than an opportunist who had acted out of ambition and, in the face of adversity, had buckled under pressure rather than accept the consequences of his actions.

So ended the attempt to persuade me to give up my post in the Assembly, and on 25 March, a majority deputy, Dr Atanas Popov, rose from his seat in the chamber and read aloud a written motion, in which he stated that 'Since Deputy Dimitâr Peshev no longer enjoys the confidence of the majority of the deputies I ask that my motion to replace him be placed on today's agenda.' That was all it said, no more, no less. This was the logical outcome I had been expecting, and so I was not surprised, just as I was not surprised that it was Popov who had been chosen to read the motion or that forty-one deputies had voted in favour of it. The motion was placed on the agenda for 30 March 1943, in other words, the earliest possible date. I tried to remain calm and to confront the situation with reasoned arguments, knowing all the while that it had already been decided that the vote was to be rushed through without debate. Obviously, it was a question of preventing public exposure of certain matters – namely, the new measures against the Jews and the government's encroachment on the Assembly's prerogatives – which could only show the government in a bad light. The last thing the government wanted was for these unpleasant questions to be aired in a public debate in which an active opposition was sure to participate with well-known positions, articulated by talented and forceful orators. One could understand why the government and especially its leader would wish to proceed in this way; what I did not know, however, was whether the chairman of the National Assembly, who was supposed to safeguard the prestige and uphold the rights and role of this institution, would accept the government's terms at the risk of violating the Assembly's own rules of order. In other words, if the chairman of the Assembly were to comply with the government's wishes, he would have to break the very rules that it was his duty to enforce – rules that had been designed to ensure the deputies' basic prerogative: their freedom to speak out on any item on the agenda. Without these rules, the Assembly made no real sense at all. A chairman could not act in this way.

Popov's motion was placed on the agenda of the National Assembly session of 30 March 1943. Presiding over the session was Christo Kalfov, and all the ministers sat around him at the table. As soon as the chairman announced that Popov's motion would be the first order of business and would be put to a vote without debate, I requested the floor so that I could ask why we were not going to be allowed to debate the motion. The chairman did not let me speak and proceeded to call a vote on the closure procedure, which would have precluded any debate. I rose in protest and stood at the foot of the speaker's rostrum, practically howling that this flagrant violation of the rules must not be allowed, that a deputy (and a member of the Assembly's leadership) was being denied his basic right of expression – an elementary right that was explicitly recognized by the rule that gave every deputy the right to speak out in his own defence, and that he was being denied that right at the very moment when he was defending himself against a vote of censure. Shouting broke out in the chamber and the scene that ensued did little to enhance the chairman's authority. If anything, it diminished it. Nevertheless, the chairman carried on, not batting an eyelid or showing himself the least bit troubled by the demeaning role he had chosen for himself, and, by extension, for the Assembly.

In the grip of my indignation, I stood at the foot of the speaker's rostrum and shouted, 'In the past, when this same Assembly debated the motion to suspend another vice-chairman, he was given the chance to defend himself, because the chairmanship was held by a worthy man.' I was referring to the censure of former vice-chairman Nikola Zakhariev in a vote that had been presided over by Alexander Malinov. On that occasion, Malinov had given the floor to Zahariev and an extensive round of debates had ensued. I, on the other hand, had not been allowed a single word in my own defence.

In the midst of all the noise, the shouting matches, the protests of deputies who demanded and were denied a chance to speak, the chairman declared that there was a majority in favour of taking up the motion without debate, as Popov had proposed, this just after having declared a majority in favour of the motion itself. Thus the meeting ended in an uproar, a storm of protests. I was censured, as the minutes of that day's meeting undoubtedly indicate. I never saw those minutes and I do not know to what extent they reflect what happened that day. I am writing all this from memory, setting down the events as I experienced them and according to my estimation of their impact on the National Assembly and the prestige of its chairman, who had allowed a member of the leadership to be violently and brutally denied the right to express himself on a question that explicitly concerned, first, the right and duty of all deputies to exercise control over the government, and, second, his personal right to self-defence and dignity.

When the dust had settled, I was convinced that, in this instance, it was the chairman of the National Assembly and the

Assembly itself that had compromised themselves in the eyes of the public, while I, on the other hand, had fulfilled my obligations.

I was glad that, now that the matter had been concluded, the anti-Jewish measures, against which our parliamentary action had been directed, were never taken up again. In fact, they were suspended almost before their implementation could begin. I do not know exactly what happened behind the scenes, but no one can deny that the end result was exactly the one that our action in the Assembly was designed to achieve. I was therefore entirely satisfied. My disappointments and my personal troubles in this story were insignificant by comparison, a mere trifle compared with the grave consequences that could have ensued if what had been commenced, and then discontinued, had been seen through to the end.

As yet, there is no detailed and accurate account of how this affair unfolded – when, where, how, and why exactly the implementation of the measures was abrogated. I do not know if we shall ever learn exactly what occurred, since nearly all the leaders of that period are now long dead. Thus we may never know the things that happened between them but left no trace. Perhaps in our own archives or in some foreign archives a document has been overlooked, but I do not now know of any. That is why the role of our action in the Assembly, or the degree to which it helped determine the course of events, cannot be established with certainty. As I have already said, I am personally convinced that our action was an important factor, because in those days the government did not dare risk a serious conflict with the National Assembly. The fact that the government took such severe, even brutal, steps to avoid any future possibility of similar actions only corroborates my supposition. The government never wanted its measures to be divulged, lest they become subject to the sort of parliamentary control we had fought to maintain.

After the war, when all that had happened during those days finally belonged to the past, it emerged that, of all the European countries under German control or influence, Bulgaria was the only one where the Jews had been rescued, where they had been spared the tragic fate that awaited the deportees. This widely acknowledged fact became an asset for Bulgaria, and would be used to great political advantage, when circumstances called for it. A diplomat, who had served as a chargé d'affaires in one of the Western countries after 9 September 1944, once admitted as much to me; in fact, he said, he himself had used this very argument in the course of his career. One can imagine what would have happened if the measures that were lifted had instead been carried out to the bitter end.

Once this whole affair had ended, I sought every opportunity to lodge a formal protest with the National Assembly against the arbitrary manner in which my vote of censure had been pursued and my not having been allowed to speak in my own defence. That opportunity finally came in December 1943, during the debates on the Assembly's budget. The moment was propitious, and I used it to protest against the chairman's violation of the most basic rules and principles of parliamentary law as well as the rights of the Assembly's deputies. I was rather vehement in my accusations, and I underscored the fact that it was he, not I, who had conducted himself in such a way as to deserve moral censure, for his actions had demeaned the Assembly. I took this opportunity to read my letter to the prime minister, from beginning to end, so that it might become part of the permanent proceedings of the National Assembly.

That was how the entire episode ended. It remains to be judged by those who are interested in the National Assembly's role in the functioning of the state.

Bibliographical Note

Numerous documents relating to the persecution of the Jews of Bulgaria were published in the *Annual* (*Godishnik*) of the Social Cultural and Educational Association of the Jews in Bulgaria, beginning in 1966. A useful, albeit tendentious, selection of these texts was published in *Oceljavaneto* (*Survival*), a compilation under the direction of David Cohen (Sofia: Shalom Publishers, 1995), with English-language summaries. Except where otherwise indicated, all the texts that appear in the present volume were drawn from that anthology and, for the most part, appear here as they do there; in general, ellipses in the text indicate deletions made by its editor.

Excerpts from Filov's diary are drawn from Bogdan Filov, *Dnevnik* (Sofia: Otechesvtven Front, 1990).

Dimo Kazasov's memoirs are drawn from several of his works.

Dimitâr Peshev's memoirs are based on a manuscript deposited in the State Archives, who have kindly made them available to us and to whom we are grateful.

The pioneer historical work on the question is still Frederick B. Chary's *The Bulgarian Jews and the Final Solution, 1940–1944* (Pittsburgh: University of Pittsburgh Press, 1974). Among the many other works on the subject, Christo Boyadjieff's *Saving the Bulgarian Jews in World War II* (Ottawa: Free Bulgarian Center, 1989) was very useful. Gabriele Nissim's *L'umo che fermo Hitler* (Milan; Mondadori, 1998) sheds a new and ample light on the role and fate of Dimitâr Peshev.

Translator's Note

This English-language version of *The Fragility of Goodness* was translated from the original French edition, which in turn was based on a number of Bulgarian sources. Mr Todorov wrote his essays and commentaries in French, and I have translated them as they appear in the original French edition of this book. As for the documents and memoirs, where partial English translations of the Bulgarian originals already existed I have referred to them and, where necessary, incorporated useful phraseology.

In the case of one of the documents, the article 'Mad Assault Against the Jews', from the *Workers' Cause* newspaper, a complete English translation was published in the *Annual* of the Social, Cultural, and Educational Association. That translation appears here essentially in its entirety.

Index

Academy of Sciences 58, 60–1
Agrarian Bank 138
Aleichem, Sholem 68
America *see* United States of
    America
Arditi, Benjamin 18
Arendt, Hannah, *Eichmann in
    Jerusalem* 1
Auschwitz 117, 122–3
Axis Alliance 5

Bagryana, E. 46, 147
Balkan Wars *see* First Balkan
    War; Second Balkan War
Bank for Bulgarian Credit 139
Banque Franco-Belge 139, 149
Banya 115
Barcelona 60
Baruch, Jose Pinkas 134
Baruch, Pinkas 134
Barukhov, Yako 134
Batak 53
Beckerle, Adolf 7–8, 12–3, 22,
    32, 84
Belev, Alexander 5, 7, 11–3, 20,
    31, 43, 71

Belgium 73
Birobijan 68
Boboshevski, Tsvyatko 106n
Bohemia 73
Boris III, King of Bulgaria:
    executive role 3–4; agrees to
    deportation of Jews from
    Sofia 11–2; dies 13, 72; as
    defender of Bulgarian
    national interests 18–24, 28;
    manipulates German
    authorities 34; attitude to
    Peshev 38–40; Workers'
    Party on 75–6; Filov discusses
    plan to send Jewish children
    to Palestine with 84–5;
    discusses 'Jewish Question'
    with Filov 86, 90–91; and
    visit to Hitler 89–90; and
    meeting of metropolitans
    90–1, 96, 102–3; Cyril sends
    protest telegram to 98;
    Mushanov and Stainov write
    to 104–5; receives letter of
    protest against Jewish
    deportations 106–7; Workers'

Cause attacks 110; Kazasov on 121; Synod sends report to 127–31

Botev, Christo 52, 66, 111

Boyadjiev, P. 49

Brannik, the (Defenders) 31, 99–100, 108, 153

Breznik 167

Buchenwald 117

Budapest 60

Buenos Aires 60

Bulgarian Lawyers' Union *see* Union of Lawyers

Bulgarian Merchants' Union 149

Bulgarian National Agrarian Union 39

Bulgarian Public Opinion and the Problems of Racism and Anti-Semitism 121

Bulgarian Students' Union 150

Bulgarian Writers' Union 32, 34, 45–6, 59n, 146–7

Bulgarian Youth League 151–2

Burgas 52

censorship bureau 59

Central Consistory of Jews 143–5

Central Cooperative Bank 138

Central Credit Cooperative 138

Chalburov, S. 87

Chary, Frederick *The Bulgarian Jews and the Final Solution* 3

Cheshmedjiev, Grigor 46, 46n 147

Chilingirov, S. 46, 147

Church, Bulgarian Orthodox: protests against deportation of Sofia Jews; defence of Jews strengthens 25, 28–9, 150; government response to protests by 35, 125; statement by 54–7; Filov on 90–1; condemns Law for the Denfence of the Nation 120; *see also* Holy Synod; Kliment, metropolitan of Stara Zagora; Cyril, metropolitan of Plovdiv; Stefan, metropolitan of Sofia; Yosif, metropolitan of Varna

Commissariat for Jewish Questions: created 7; directs attempts at deportation of Jews 71, 122; Synod on 97; begins moves to deport Sofia Jews 106; complaints about 154; Peshev on 159, 161–3

Communist Party 14, 16–7, 26, 65n, 71, 120, 122

Communists 18, 39–40, 84–5; *see also* Communist Party; Workers' Party

Congress of Minorities, the 144

Consistory of Jews *see* Central Consistory of Jews

Craftsmen Association 34

Credit Bank 139

Croatia 94

Cyril, metropolitan of Plovdiv (*later* Patriarch of Bulgaria) 10, 25, 40, 98

Dachau 117–9
Dannecker, Theodor, SS
 Hauptsturmführer 7–8, 11–2,
 20, 71, 162n
Danube, the (river) 83, 122, 126
Djerov, Nikolla 46
Dobrudja 3–4, 51n, 177n
Dubrovnik 60
Dupnitsa 81, 99–100, 122, 126,
 158
Durov, Dr 88

Eden, Anthony (*later* Sir
 Anthony, 1st Earl of Avon) 6
Ehrenburg, Ilya 69
Eichmann, Karl Adolf 7, 11, 71
Elin-Pelin 46, 59, 120, 147
England *see* Great Britain

Fatherland Front, the *see*
 Otechesvtven Front
Ferdinand, King of Bulgaria 76
Filipov, Nikola 46
Filov, Bogdan: assures Germans
 of readiness for Jewish
 deporations 7; reaction to
 Peshev's protest 10–11, 37–8;
 effect of Allied landings on
 deportation plans of 13;
 Rédard has meeting with 20,
 92–4, 71–2; misconception of
 consequences of Jewish
 deportations 27; and
 Kazasov's open letter 35,
 58–61; and Bulgarian political
 order 40; Peshev heads letter
 of protest against Jewish

deportation to 78–9; Stainov
 sends Interrogatory to 81–3;
 diary entries on Jewish
 deportations 84–91, 95;
 Stainov pleads with for repeal
 of anti–Jewish legislation 104;
 Workers' Cause attacks 110;
 Synod intercedes with 128–9;
 as Freemason 142; and
 Peshev's letter of protest
 169–76
First Balkan War 51n, 176n
France 4, 73
Freemasons 142

Gabrovski, Petâr: announces
 anti-Jewish legislation 5, 43;
 assures Germans of readiness
 for Jewish deportations 7;
 disavows knowledge of arrests
 10; agrees to suspend
 deportation orders 19; and
 Peshev's insistence that
 deportations stop 35–7; Filov
 discusses Lukov assassination
 with 85; discusses 'Jewish
 Question' with king 90; and
 Kyunstendil delegation 137;
 as Freemason 143; on need to
 end dissent over 'Jewish
 Question' 155; demands copy
 of Peshev letter 168
Genov, Minko 46
Georgiev, Serafim 88
German-Soviet Pact 4
Germany: membership of Axis
 5; racial legislation in 43; and

the 'Jewish question' 68–9;
consequences of defeat of
79n; Bulgarian workers in 86;
Filov pleads lack of
manpower in 93; as source of
Bulgarian inflation 111; and
Nazi claims of Jewish-
influenced press 140; anti-
Jewish measures in 147–8;
Peshev reluctant to
antagonise 167
Goebbels, Joseph 20
Gorianski, P. 46
Gorky, Maxim (*ps of* Alexei
Maksimovich Peshkov) 67
Gorna Djumaya 81, 122
Great Britain 23, 76
Greece 3, 5, 73, 90, 122, 176n
Gruev, P. 127, 129
Guela, the 144

Hananel, Dr, Chief Rabbi
126–7
Hitler, Adolf: Boris III visits 21,
89–90; demands that Bulgaria
surrender Jews 23; loses
restraint 73–4; Workers'
Party attacks 76, 109, 111;
Kazasov on 117, 121–2;
Stefan urges Boris to distance
himself from policies of 130
Hoffmann, Karl 7, 11, 19
Holland 73
Holy Synod, the 97–103, 125;
see also Church, Bulgarian
Orthodox; Kliment,
metropolitan of Stara Zagora;

Cyril, metropolitan of
Plovdiv; Stefan, metropolitan
of Sofia; Yosif, metropolitan
of Varna
Hungary 4, 73–4

Ikonomov, Dimitâr 9, 14, 21,
28–30, 35, 40, 158–9, 161
Ikonomov N. P. 46
Isaev, Mladen 46
Israel 16, 18, 26, 116
Italy 5, 68

Japan 5
Jekov, General Nikola 75, 111
Jews: distribution of population
in Bulgaria 4, 31–2; race laws
against enacted 4–7, 43–4;
denied Bulgarian citizenship
in Macedonia and Thrace
5–6; deported from Thrace
and Macedonia 7–9, 11, 14,
16, 20, 30, 71, 92–3, 97–8,
100, 107, 122, 126, 132, 157;
deportation from 'old
Bulgaria' blocked 10–13, 30,
38–9, 97–8, 125, 136, 162,
164–7, 177, 182; in Sofia 12,
43; race laws against repealed
13; attitude to fallen public
figures 15; exodus from
Bulgaria to Israel 16; king's
attitude to deportation of
16–24; exclusion from
Bulgarian society 43; attempts
to deport 43, 71–93, 104–7;

Filov on 84–91; Stefan on
treatment of 100–1; as
'profiteers' 102–3; 110–1,
135, 150–7; Workers' Party
publicises treatment of
108–10; in Dachau 117–9;
terror of 132–3; position in
commercial credit system
138–9, 144, 149; as traders
139–40, 145; position in
professional life 140; and
definition of 'Jewish origins'
155; Peshev on treatment of
158
Jivkov, Todor 17–8

Kalfov, Christo 87, 167–8, 180
Kamenova, Ana 46
Karadja, Stefan 110
Karavelov, Petko 100n
Karavelova, Ekaterina 100
Katowice 9
Kazasov, Dimo: in position of
power 15; courage and wit of
35, 40; signatory of Punev
open letter 53; open letter to
Filov 58–61; signatory of
open letter to king 106n;
sources of memoirs 115–6;
visit to Dachau 117–9; on
resistance to anti-Jewish
legislation 119–24; writes to
Filov on effects of anti–Jewish
legislation 147
Kiev 68
Kirladjiev, Tsindy 133

Kishinev 68
Kliment, metropolitan of Stara
Zagora 25
Kocherinovo 126
Kojukharov, Todor 88, 167
Konstantinov, K. 46
Kosturkov, Stoyan 53
Kunchev (fascist leader) 138
Kunev, Trifon 46, 147
Kurtev, Vladimir 133, 135, 160
Kvitko, Lev 69
Kyoseivanov, Petâr 87–8
Kyustendil 9–10, 30, 81, 99,
116, 132–3, 135–6, 160–2

Law for the Defence of the
Nation: introduced in
legislature 4; rescinded 13;
Petrov fights against 15;
Communist protests against
dismissed 18; public protest
against 23; Peshev opposes
25–7; Peshev votes in favour
of 29; widespread opposition
to 34; nature of reactions to
43–4; Bulgarian Writers'
Union protests against 45–6;
Bulgarian Lawyers' Union
protests against 47–9;
opposition protests against
50–3; Church protests against
54–7; Stainov speaks against
62–4; Poliakov speaks against
65–9; as catalyst for Jewish
conversions 99; Stefan on
101; Synod on 103; Kazasov
on resistance to 119–24;

Peshev on passage of 137–84

Lawyers' Union *see* Union of Lawyers

Legionnaires, the 31, 99n

Leonov, Buko 136

Levski, Vasil 52, 110

Ligi, David 15

Liliev, Nikolai 46, 147

Lom 9, 81–2, 122

Lukov, Christo 84

Macedonia: Bulgaria loses 3, 176n; Bulgaria assumes control of 5; Jews deported from 7–9, 11, 14, 16, 20, 71, 92–3, 97–8, 100, 107, 122, 132, 157; Bulgarian occupation of 23; Bulgarian minority in 48n; Stainov questions deportation of Jews from 81–3; Bulgaria expects restoration of rule over 148n

Majdanek 117, 122

Malinov, Alexander 181

Marinov, Spas 87

Markish, Perets 69

Marshak, Samuel 69

Mauthausen 117

Mevorakh, Nissim 15

Midilov, P. 142

Mikhalev, Petâr: as part of delegation from Kyustendil 10; given life sentence by People's Tribunal 15; pressures Grabovski 35; on Peshev 115; honoured at Yad Vashem 116n; protests against Jewish deportations 133, 135–6; lobbies minister about anti-Jewish legislation 161

Mikhov, Nikola 85

Miltenov (Kyustendil assistant chief of police) 132–3

Minev, Miroslav 46

Mitov, D. B. 46

Momchilov, I. 133, 135, 160

Moscow 68

Mushanov, Nikola 95, 104–5, 106n

Munich 117

National Awakening, the 63

Neftyanov, Konstantin 53

Neofit of Vidin, Grand Vicar and President of the Holy Synod 54–7, 90–91, 97n

Nissim, Gabriele 24

Nobel Peace Prize 17

North Africa 12

Norway 73

Nuremberg race laws 4

Oceljavaneto (anthology) 18, 21, 115

Odessa 68

opposition: non-Communist 53n, 58n, 62n

Otechesvtven Front (the Fatherland Front; newspaper) 39, 71, 73–4, 111

Ottoman Empire 32

Paisi, metropolitan 90–91

Palestine: Bulgarian Jews
attempt flight to 6; Rédard
seeks to negotiate departure
of Jewish children to 72;
Filov on plan to send Jewish
children to 84–7; Rédard
seeks admission of Jews to 92;
pre-war Bulgarian Jewish
emigration to 144
Partov, Dr K. 177–8
Pasternak, Boris 69
Pastukhov, K. 106n
Pazardjik 81
Pearl Harbor 5
Pen Club 58–9
People's Bank 139
People's Tribunal 14–5, 116,
173n
Peshev, Dimitâr: on reactions to
anti-Jewish legislation 5; and
attempt to deport Jews from
'Old Bulgaria' 9–11;
sentenced by People's
Tribunal 14–6; context of
actions of 24–6; motives for
actions 28–30; strategy 35–9;
consequences of action 71;
open letter to Filov 78–80;
Filov receives petition from
86–7; Filov calls for vote of
censure on 88–9; accounts of
115; writes memoirs 116;
protests against deportation
of Jews 123; and Kyustendil
delegation 134–6; on passage
of Law for the Defence of the
Nation 137–84

Petkov, Nikola 39, 106n
Petkov, Tsvyatko 161
Petrich 52
Petrov, Ivan V. 14
Pirot 8
Plovdiv 81, 98–9, 133, 136
Poland 72, 73, 86, 90, 92, 122,
125–6
Polyakov, Todor 65–9
Popov, Dr Atanas 89, 179–80
Popov (waiter) 133
Prague 60
Punev, Christo 50–3

Rabotnichesko Delo (the Workers'
Cause) 95, 108–12
Radio Moscow 73–4
Raichev, N. 49
Ratnik, the (Guardians) 5, 31,
99n
Rédard, Charles 20, 27–8, 72,
85–6, 92–4
Rennes 86
Ribbentrop, Joachim von 21–2,
89–90
Rila 125
Romania 3–4, 94, 122
Runevski, Ivan 53
Rusaliev, V. 46
Ruse 52, 136
Russo-Turkish Wars 32, 76n

Sakâzov, Yanko 53
Samokov 99
Schmidt, Paul 85
Second Balkan War 3, 176n
Semerdjiev, Georgi 'Truntata'
133

Serbia 3, 73, 176n
Sevov, Yordan 87
Sicily 13
Simeon, Crown Prince 13
Simonet, Jacques 133
Skopje 132
Slaveikov, Pencho 65
Slovakia 94
Social, Cultural and Educational
    Organization of the Jews in
    Bulgaria 16
Sofia: Jewish population in
    12–3, 99–101, 108n; anti-
    Jewish rumours in 52;
    deportation of Jews from 106,
    108–12, 127; Suichmezov
    takes refuge in 136;
    distribution of Jewish
    professionals in 144–5
Sofia District Committee of the
    Workers' Party 71, 75–7
Sofroni, metropolitan 21, 90
Soviet Union *see* Union of
    Socialist Soviet Republics
Spain 90
Stainov, Petko: reaction to
    Jewish deportees 9; in
    position of power 15; makes
    public protestations 21; and
    anti-Jewish discrimination 31;
    courage of 40; signatory to
    Punev letter 53; speech to
    National Assembly 62–4; and
    deportations of Jews from
    Thrace and Macedonia 71;
    Interrogatory sent by 81–3;

on Filov 89; and report to
    king 95; letter to king 104–5
Stalin, Josef 13
Stalingrad, Battle of 12
Stanishev, Alexander 135
Stefan, metropolitan of Sofia:
    reaction to condition of
    Jewish deportees 9; receives
    Chief Rabbi 12; relieved of
    responsibilities 15; writes to
    king 20–21; outspoken on
    treatment of Jews 25; on
    treatment of Jews 29; as man
    of conscience and courage 40;
    Filov on 90–91; contribution
    to meeting of Holy Synod
    99–101; post-war fate of 115;
    protests against deportation
    of Jews 125–32
Stoyanov, Lyudmil 46
Suichmezov, Asen 10, 31,
    115–6, 132–6, 160
Svetlov, Mikhail 69
Sweden 73
Synod, the *see* Holy Synod, the

Tadjer, Colonel Avram 136
Thrace: Bulgaria assumes
    control of 5; Jews deported
    from 7–9, 11, 14, 16, 20, 30,
    71, 92–3, 97–8, 100, 107,
    122, 126, 132, 157; Bulgarian
    occupation of 23; Bulgarian
    minority in 48n; Stainov
    questions deportation of Jews
    from 81–3; Bulgaria expects
    restoration of rule over 148n;

Bulgaria loses 176n
Todt Organizations 93
Treblinka 9
Troyan 136
Tsankov, Alexander 89n,111,
  121, 167
Tsankovite Movement, the 120
Tsion, Rabbi Daniel 18, 127
Turkey 33, 76

Union of Artists' Societies 34
Union of Cooperative Banks
  138
Union of Doctors 34, 147
Union of Lawyers 28, 34, 47–9,
  145–6
Union of Socialist Soviet
  Republics (Soviet Union) 68
United States of America 5, 23,
  76

Vasilev, Slaveiko 87
Vazov, Ivan cit. 45
Vazov, Ivan 65

Velchev, Damyan 106n
Vidin 52
Vienna 9, 122
Vlaikov, T. G. 46, 59, 147
Volen, Ilia 46

Workers' Cause, the see
  Rabotnichesko Delo
Workers' Party 17; see also
  Communist Party; Sofia
  District Committee of the
  Workers' Party
Writers' Union see Bulgarian
  Writers' Union

Yad Vashem (Israel) 116
Yanev, Sotir 88
Yasharov, Yosif 15–6
Yavorov, Peyo 65
Yosif, metropolitan of Varna 25
Yugoslavia 5, 122

Zakhariev, Nikola 181